Health Craft

❖ ❖ ❖

Waterless
& Greaseless
Cooking

Manufacturers of the world's
finest cookware.

© Copyright 1995 by
Vita Craft Corporation
11100 W. 58th Street
Shawnee, Kansas 66203

ISBN 0-9648-421-1-4

Editor	**CHERI SPARKS** **VITA CRAFT CORPORATION**
Recipe Selection, Food Styling & Design	**CHERI SPARKS** **& JANET LEE**
Food Photography	**BOB GRIER & ASSOCIATES**
Graphic Design	**KAREN BENTON DESIGN**
Nutritional Analysis	**ANN HUNTER, PhD, RD,** **LD, FADA**
Printing	**ROSSE LITHOGRAPHING** **COMPANY**

HEALTH CRAFT
5 PLY NICROMIUM SURGICAL STEEL
MADE IN U.S.A.
TAMPA, FL 1-813-885-5244

From the time I was in high school I've always wanted to be a Chef. Today I have the pleasure of appearing weekly on the "Harris & Company Show" broadcast by NBC affiliate WFLA TV; soon, we hope to be a national broadcast from Busch Gardens in Tampa. This affiliation began with my love for cooking, coupled with my 25 year history in the cookware industry. I began my career as a salesman for another cookware company and in 1983 my wife, LeAnn, and I started our own company, Health Craft.

Health Craft today is a multimillion-dollar company whose people are dedicated to serving customers just like you. Our success is due to our belief in our products, our adherence to quality standards, and our mission to bring you the finest cooking utensils available today; as well as accurate information on health, fitness, and nutrition.

LeAnn and I personally designed the newest collection, Gold Classic. Like our other products, it is constructed with care of the finest materials and craftsmanship, making it both beautiful and functional. We are proud of our products, and I trust you will enjoy your cookware during the preparation of your meals throughout your lifetime.

Charles Knight, President

TABLE OF CONTENTS

Ann Hunter, PhD, RD, LD, FADA
Wichita State University

Now that you've invested in a set of Health Craft cookware, it's time to reap the many rewards— hassle-free cooking, delicious meals, and improved health. I know through my years of experience in the food service industry that nothing detracts more from a pleasurable cooking experience than not having the right food to prepare or the right equipment to work with.

As a dietitian, I want my finished entrees to appeal to the eye and the palate, and to meet my clients' nutritional needs. Overcooked vegetables that have lost their color and flavor have little to no nutritional value. Dried out meats that have lost their flavor, are difficult to chew and swallow. With the Health Craft Nutritional Cooking System, you can rest assured that these cooking nightmares won't happen to you. Health Craft cookware retains the valuable vitamins and minerals as well as the natural moisture in your foods.

Because we understand your lifestyle needs, much care went into the selection of the recipes in this cookbook. We recommend you reference the nutritional breakdown of each recipe. For a complete explanation of this breakdown, see page 13. In addition to including the most nutritious entrees, Health Craft has made your variety of choices almost limitless. Choose from a variety of irresistible recipes, such as Singapore Fish, Chicken Satay, Hom Bow, and even Chocolate Mousse.

Part of my role has been determining the nutritional information for each recipe, but through the process I've lived, tasted, and visualized each meal personally. During this project, recipes were improved by reducing fat, sodium, and caloric count, while increasing fiber whenever possible. All this was done without sacrificing the appearance, texture, or taste of the dishes. Each recipe was then retested for taste, quality, and accurate preparation instructions.

So much has been written about nutrition, cholesterol, fats, and diets during the past ten years, it's no wonder we sometimes feel bombarded with information. That's why in this cookbook we've gotten back to the basics of nutrition. You should find the following sections particularly useful: The Surgeon General's report as it relates to foods and nutrition; the Food Guide Pyramid; the basics of metabolism and fats; the new food labels and how to use them; and the calorie point system. We hope you'll turn to these reference pages for years to come.

I've enjoyed my Health Craft cookware for many years and still continue to learn new ways to prepare foods—without added fats and water. You will too!

Easily prepared, nutritional meals that are appealing to the eye and the palate—what more could you ask for?

Congratulations on your decision to purchase the Health Craft Nutritional Cooking System. Your decision will pay lifelong dividends in healthful, flavorful and nutritional foods. The vapor seal method of cooking assures you of maximum food value retention, and allows you to prepare your foods without water or added fats. Take a moment now to acquaint yourself with the proper use and care of these fine utensils. By following a few simple steps you will enjoy the maximum benefits and become an expert with the Health Craft Nutritional Cooking System.

Wash Before Using

Before using the cookware, wash each piece thoroughly in one-half cup vinegar and hot, soapy water. This initial washing is essential to insure that all manufacturing oils are removed before cooking food. After this initial washing, normal washing by hand or in a dishwasher is all that is necessary to clean your cookware.

Daily Care

After each use, wash your cookware in warm soapy water with a dish cloth or nylon plastic net. Do not use metal scouring pads, as they will scratch the surface of the cookware. Your cookware may also be placed in the dishwasher.

Discoloration

Occasionally, when cooking starchy foods or searing meats a stain may appear on the inside surface of the pan. A blue or golden brown discoloration may also appear on the outside of the pan from overheating the unit. These stains are easily removed with a good non-abrasive stainless steel cleaner. First, make a paste with the cleaner and water. Then, using a paper towel or cloth rub the paste over the stained area, rinse and dry.

Burned Foods

If burned foods are not easily removed by normal washing, fill the pan with hot water and let it soak. If the food particles are still stuck, fill the pan partially full of water and bring it to a boil long enough to loosen the food.

Surface Care

While stainless steel is an extremely durable metal, it is not impervious to corrosion, pitting or spotting. Foods such as mustard, mayonnaise, lemon juice, tomatoes, tomato paste, vinegar, salt, dressings, or condiments may etch stainless steel if allowed to remain in contact with the surface for a long period of time. Strong bleaches can have the same effect.

Pitting may result if undissolved salt is allowed to remain on the bottom of the pan. Pitting looks like small white spots. This pitting does not in any way affect the performance or usefulness of your pans, nor are they a defect in the metal or the workmanship. To avoid pitting, salt should only be added to boiling liquid and stirred until it is completely dissolved.

Dried Fruits

Do not cover sulphur dried foods or foods labeled sulphites added as it may stain the cover. Boil liquid for 10 minutes prior to covering when cooking these foods.

Mother nature designed food to give us everything we need—naturally. Food contains abundant flavor, vitamins, minerals, digestive enzymes, and color. However, many cooking methods can rob food of its natural qualities.

Fortunately, Health Craft's vapor seal, waterless, greaseless cookware saves money, work, time, energy, flavor, vitamins, minerals and enzymes.

"Waterless, greaseless" cooking is possible because a vapor seal is created around the lid; and heat is distributed evenly across the bottom and up the sides of the cookware.

This process cooks food in its own natural liquids for nutritious, flavor-filled meals. Food shrinkage is greatly reduced, making waterless, greaseless cooking more economical than ordinary cooking methods. The vapor seal is maintained by using low heat. Thus, Health Craft is the most energy efficient cookware on the market.

The vapor seal method retains the nutritional value of your food by eliminating the following processes that drain food of its natural goodness. Peeling fruits and vegetables removes the vitamins and minerals directly beneath the skin. We do not recommend you peel these foods; a good scrub is all that is necessary.

Boiling sterilizes food, dissolves water soluble minerals, and destroys both the flavor and color. The vapor seal method cooks food completely in its own natural moisture, without added water and without boiling.

High temperature destroys vitamins and minerals and causes food shrinkage. For example, when you smell a roast cooking in the oven you are really smelling the natural meat juices that have been transformed into vapor. The high temperature combined with open cooking greatly adds to meat shrinkage. The vapor seal method cooks meats on medium to low heat, retaining the natural juices which tenderize and flavor the meat. This method also retains the natural juices and flavor and greatly decreases meat shrinkage.

Oxidation of food occurs when cooking without a cover exposes food to the air, greatly reducing the quality of the food. These qualities are locked into food when the vapor seal is formed, keeping the aroma in the pan. For example, you will not know if broccoli or cabbage is being cooked until the cover is removed from the pan.

Lastly, grease—adding fats and oils in food preparation makes food seven times harder to digest, as well as adding excessive calories. Using the vapor seal, the foods' natural properties keep them from sticking. Plus, the vapor seal retains natural flavors. The need for added butter and oils after cooking is not necessary to restore flavor.

Vapor seal cooking is very different from traditional cooking because you do not need to add moisture or fats. Everything else you already know about cooking applies, once you know the vapor seal basics.

The Simple Basic Rules

Always use the correct size pan, one that the food most nearly fills. Cooking with a pan too large for the food quantity can destroy vitamins and minerals, dry your foods, and possibly cause your food to burn.

Create a Vapor Seal

Fill a pan with fresh or frozen vegetables. Rinse in cold water then drain. Enough water clings to the food to combine with natural juices to cook food in its own moisture. Cover the pan, close vent, place on a burner, and turn burner to low. When lid is hot to the touch and the lid can be spun freely, the vapor seal has formed. Continue cooking on low until done. This is the waterless part of this new cooking. If you cook several vegetables together with no water there will be no interchange of flavor. Each vegetable will be full of its own flavor and valuable nutrients.

> The vapor seal retains the moisture in your foods with a water seal around the inset of the pan. Sometimes when a pan is allowed to cool, the condensed moisture inside the pan creates a vacuum causing the lid to lock onto the pan. Should this happen, simply open the vent.

Control the Heat

Waterless, greaseless cooking is a low-temperature method that can be used on any type of stove. Lower heat retains moisture and keeps food from burning. The following are general rules for heat use.

MEDIUM-HIGH HEAT
- For heating utensils to brown or sear meat
- For re-moisturizing dried foods by steaming over water *until* the water boils
- For pan broiling thick steaks or chops (¾" or thicker)

MEDIUM HEAT
- For pan broiling thin steaks, chops, hamburgers or chicken breasts
- For starting fresh fruits and vegetables until vapor seal forms
- To start direct top-of-range baking

LOW (OR SIMMER) HEAT
- For cooking roasts after browning
- For cooking fresh vegetables and fruits after vapor seal forms
- For re-moisturizing dried foods by steaming over water *after* the water boils
- For cooking less tender cuts of meat after browning all sides
- For finishing top-of-range baking after pan cover is hot

Don't Peek

Resist that urge to peek: When the cover is removed during the cooking period, heat and moisture are allowed to escape and the vapor seal is broken. This lengthens cooking time.

Be Specific

Follow time charts, recipes and general instructions for meats, vegetables, etc., under their specific headings.

Cooking Meats without Grease

Begin with meat at room-temperature. Pre-heat your pan on medium for 3-5 minutes. The pan is ready when you can sprinkle a few drops of water in the pan and they "dance." If the water just evaporates, the pan is not hot enough. Once the pan is hot, place the meat in the pan, pressing it against the bottom of the pan. The meat will stick at first, which is what is required. After a short time, the meat will sear and then loosen from the pan. When this happens, turn and sear the other side. If meat is not done, or if it is a roast, cover the pan and reduce heat to low until cooked.

Tip: Always roast your meat in the smallest unit into which the meat will fit. This will result in more tender, juicy meat. Also, the meat will shrink less, which allows more servings per pound and greater money savings.

Top-of-the-Range-Baking

Health Craft's design allows you to bake cakes and cornbreads in the pan on top of the stove more efficiently than in the oven. For example, to bake a small cake, take the 8½" fry pan and coat the inside with a non-stick cooking spray. Then pour the cake batter into the pan until the pan is half full, and cover with the lid. Set the pan on a burner and adjust heat to medium. When the lid is hot to the touch (usually about five minutes), reduce heat to low and finish baking (usually 10-12 minutes).

Stack Cooking

All Health Craft pans are designed to work together. Stack cooking is one of the ways they do. It is an exciting and very efficient benefit of Health Craft cookware. And it's something you simply cannot do with most other cookware!

Stack cooking lets you prepare more foods at one time by stacking small utensils on top of larger utensils on one burner. This is possible because of Health Craft's exceptional heat conductivity, which transfers heat across the bottom and up the sides of the cookware. The high dome cover is made of the same multi-ply material making the perfect surface for stack cooking.

Here's an example of stack cooking:

• Begin cooking a roast as normal in the six-quart roaster; sear it on all sides then place accompanying vegetables around it.
• Lower the heat and set the steamer rack in the roaster. Put prepared cake mix in the double boiler, cover tightly with foil, and set on steamer rack. Cover with high dome cover.
• Pre-heat a small pan of frozen vegetables or cored apples on medium heat until lid is hot to the touch. Then turn off the burner under the small vegetable pan and set pan on top of the dome cover to continue cooking.
This whole meal will cook in about 50 minutes – on one burner!

Health Craft's five-ply and nine-ply cookware are composed of multiple layers of pure aluminum and aluminum alloy covered inside and out with the finest surgical stainless steel. (The nine-ply features additional layers of ferritic and stainless steel.) The aluminum is a light weight metal and an excellent conductor of heat allowing efficient use of energy while cooking. It spreads heat evenly to prevent hot spots that make food stick or burn. The stainless steel is an alloy combining iron and other elements to create a hard surface that is durable, resistant to wear, easy to clean, sanitary, and can be highly polished for an attractive, permanent finish. Health Craft also produces cookware for magnetic induction ranges.

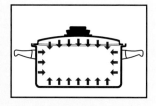

Even Heat Distribution
Heat is distributed across the bottom and up the sides of the cookware.

Our Outstanding Features

Beyond its vapor seal advantages, Health Craft cookware is designed with every concern of the modern kitchen user in mind.

Self-storing covers: The lids, when inverted, nest perfectly in the pan for easy storage. No searching for the right lid – it's with the pan.

Burn-safe knobs and finger guards: The knob rests on a finger guard that prevents your fingers from touching the hot lid. Both the knob and guard are made of heat resistant materials – oven safe to 400° (on "bake"). The knob also has a brass fitting, not plastic, so it does not expand and strip. The handles and knobs are also dishwasher safe.

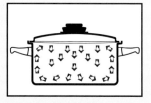

Waterless Cooking
The vapor seal keeps all the natural goodness of food inside the pan.

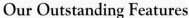

Handle fitting: The handle is protected by the stainless steel flame guard between the handle and the pan. Attachment by stainless steel weld ensures stability and stay tight handle in locked position. The knob has a brass insert for longevity and cleanability. Handles and knobs are safe to 350°F.

No rivets or rolled edges: No rivets penetrate the inside of the pans. Grease and food particles can be trapped around rivets, making such a pan design much more difficult to clean. Also, our pans are easier to clean because they do not have rolled edges on the top rim.

Warp resistant bottom: The bottom of the pan is designed to assure the utensil hugs the burner for maximum heating efficiency. This feature makes Health Craft cookware practical for all types of ranges, including smooth glass top surface ranges.

Vapor Vent: Cook chicken, steaks and chops to a beautiful crisp golden brown with the lid on and vent open. Cook vegetables in their own juices to save vitamins and minerals with the vent closed.

The recipes in this cookbook are U.S. standard measurements. Appropriate metric equivalents are also provided within each recipe. For small quantities, customary tablespoon and teaspoon measurements are used in the recipes.

For easy reference, the following metric conversions have been rounded to provide convenient working measurements.

Weight

U.S.	Metric
1 ounce	30 grams
4 ounce	115 grams
8 ounce	230 grams
16 ounces (1 pound)	460 grams
32 ounces (2 pounds)	1 kilogram

Oven Temperature

U.S.	Metric
200°F	90°C
225°F	110°C
250°F	120°C
275°F	135°C
300°F	150°C
350°F	180°C
375°F	190°C
400°F	210°C

Imperial/Australian Equivalents

Other	Metric
1 Imperial ½ pint (10 oz)	300 ml
1 Australian cup (8 oz)	240 ml

Note: 1¼ U.S. cup (10 oz) =
1 Imperial ½ pint

Volume Measures

U.S.	Metric
teaspoon to milliliter	
¼ teaspoon	1.5 ml
½ teaspoon	3 ml
1 teaspoon	5 ml
1½ teaspoons	7.5 ml
2 teaspoons	10 ml
2½ teaspoons	12.5 ml
tablespoon to milliliter	
1 tablespoon	15 ml
1½ tablespoons	22.5 ml
2 tablespoons	30 ml
cup to milliliter	
¼ cup	60 ml
⅓ cup	80 ml
½ cup	120ml
⅔ cup	160 ml
¾ cup	180 ml
1 cup	240 ml
4 cups (1 quart)	1 liter

Each recipe provides you quick, at-a-glance information, in the same place on every recipe. This feature allows you to quickly see all the information you need. For instance, preparation time is the second feature for every recipe. If you have surprise guests for dinner, or you need to be somewhere else – this feature lets you know quickly if you have enough time to prepare the recipe.

Number of servings: If the recipe makes enough for eight and you know you need only four, divide all ingredients in half before preparing.

Utensil: The proper utensil is called for in every recipe. Never again will you be pouring from one pot to another because there is not enough room in the first utensil.

Ingredients: everything you need is in one column – no searching necessary. Additionally all ingredients are listed for U.S. and metric measures when appropriate, making converting unnecessary.

Preparation: Short, to-the-point descriptions of each step.

Nutritional Breakdown: Any way you measure your nutritional needs – by calories, by grams, by percent of the total or the calorie point system – it can be found. Always in the same order, always in the same place.

Recipe Symbol Explanation

The A, C, Calcium, and Iron boxes are for quick, at-a-glance reference as is the pie chart feature. Dietary analysis was used to determine these values. The pie chart in the lower left indicates the percentage of calories derived from fat (F/G), protein (P), and carbohydrates (C) for a particular recipe. The colored bar symbols for Vitamin A, Vitamin C, Calcium, and Iron will be visible in the lower right for recipes that provide at least 20% of your daily value of these nutrients.

Example of nutritional information

NUTRITIONAL BREAKDOWN PER SERVING
Calories 280
Fat Grams 13
Carbohydrate Grams 19
Protein Grams 21
Cholesterol mg 52
Sodium mg 473
THE POINT SYSTEM
Calorie Points 3$\frac{1}{2}$
Protein Points 3
Fat Grams 13
Sodium Points 20$\frac{1}{2}$
Fiber Points 1
Carbohydrate Points 1$\frac{1}{2}$
Cholesterol Points 5

P
F/G　C

A
C
CALCIUM CALCIO
IRON HIERRO

Method used for nutritional information was Nutritionist IV software, N-Square Computing and *Food Values of Portions Commonly Used* by Jean A.T. Pennington.

Many cooks put a lot of pressure on themselves when it comes to preparing a meal. They must have a recipe to follow and it must be followed to the tee. Although the stores are full of cookbooks, there are not many on waterless/greaseless cooking. To be able to enjoy the recipes available and receive the benefits of cooking without water and added fats, you will need to learn to adapt recipes. The easiest way to do this is to understand and trust your cookware.

Use Lower Temperature Settings

One of the benefits of Health Craft cookware is the way it conducts heat – on low. One common mistake is using a heat setting that is too high. Keep this in mind – a perfect cake can bake in Health Craft on top of the range on LOW. To bake the same cake in the oven would require 350°F (180°C)! The full body construction of the multi-core goes across the bottom and up the sides of the pan, conducting heat evenly, requiring lower temperatures. Think of a pan and cover as a mini-oven on top of your stove. Leave the cover in place,

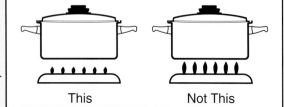

This   Not This

the same as you leave an oven door shut. To bake cakes, spray the pan with non-stick cooking spray (or lightly grease) – fill the pan half full with batter, and cover. Start cooking on medium heat for five minutes, then reduce to low heat. Cook according to time listed on recipe directions.

Understanding Waterless Cooking

Rinse and freshen vegetables. Pour off excess water, cover utensil, close vent, set on low heat, and remember not to peek. Every time you raise the cover you allow the moisture to escape. Be sure you are using the correct pan. The vegetables should fill or almost fill the pan. Too much air is like a sauna in a ballroom – it does not work.

If the food has moisture like vegetables you can retain the moisture — if it is dried, such as rice, pasta, or dried beans, you will need to add some water.

Enjoy Greaseless Cooking

You may prepare your foods WITHOUT added oils and fats. Remember, you are cooking on a stainless steel surface. To prepare steaks, preheat the utensil on medium to medium-high heat until water drops "dance" when sprinkled in the pan. Place steaks in the pan (take care in placing your steaks as they will immediately begin to sear, temporarily sticking to the surface, and you should not move them until they are ready to turn). After 4-5 minutes try to lift a corner of your steak, do not force, the meat releases itself. When that side is seared, turn and cook to your steak preference.

To sauté onions and garlic, simply use low heat, cover pan, and close vent — they sauté in their own moisture...no oil is needed. If olive oil is added, it's added for the flavor so often less is used. Most meats, chicken, chops, and fish have natural fats and oils, so you do not need to add them. Eggs have no natural oil — you need to spray the pan with vegetable cooking spray or use a small amount of butter or margarine.

Practice Regular Cleaning

Use a stainless steel cleaner regularly. Your Health Craft cookware performs best when very clean.

Roasting Beef and Lamb

Begin with meat at room temperature. To roast beef, preheat appropriate size pan over medium heat. Sear first side of meat, partially cover pan or cover with vent open. After first side is seared turn meat and reduce heat to low. With the high dome cover in place, roast to desired doneness. Proper cooking temperature can be determined by small bubbles forming around the base of the high dome cover. If water bubbles are spitting, reduce temperature. Cooking time begins after turning and covering meat.

Minutes per pound	Desired doneness	Internal Temperature*
8	Rare	
9	Medium-Rare	145°F (65°C)
10	Medium	165°F (70°C)
11	Medium-Well	
12	Well	170°F (75°C)

*Internal cooking temperatures established by USDA

Pan Broiling

Preheat appropriate size frypan without grease over medium-high heat until water drops "dance" on pan. Place meats in pan lightly pressing down to ensure surface is in contact with pan. Partially cover pan or cover with vent open. Meat will immediately begin to sear, initially sticking to the pan. When first side is seared (3-4 minutes) meats will loosen, turn over and sear second side an additional 3-4 minutes.

To deglaze the pan for sauce; after removing meats add ⅓ cup (80 ml) of liquid (water, wine, broth, etc.) and stir to loosen the juices from pan. Pour over steaks on platter.

Pan-Frying

Pan frying is recommended for thin steaks such as cube steaks, or floured and breaded meats. Add a little oil or shortening prior to adding floured meats to the pan.

Steaming Meats

An excellent way to remove the fat from ground beef and other ground meats, is by steaming in place of browning or frying the meat. Place steamer over boiling water, add ground beef to steamer and cover. Frequently remove cover to stir ground beef. Sausage and hot dogs also benefit from this method.

Roasting Poultry

Cooking time is for unstuffed, skinned poultry. Start cooking on medium heat, with high dome cover in place. Proper cooking temperature can be determined by small bubbles forming around the base of the high dome cover. If water bubbles are spitting, reduce temperature. When vapor seal is formed, reduce to low heat and cook all poultry for 10 minutes per pound.

Vegetables

Wash and remove blemishes. Do not peel unless recipe calls for it, for by doing so you lose food value. Place vegetables in the pan they most nearly fill. Do not defrost frozen vegetables. Freshen vegetables in water to bring back the natural moisture content and garden crispness, then drain.

Potatoes are usually cooked whole and must be thoroughly dried before cooking. If cut into halves or quarters to shorten cooking time, place skin side against the utensil. Add ¼ cup (60 ml) water as some of the starch will settle to the bottom of the pan requiring the additional water. A slightly higher temperature is required for potatoes than other vegetables.

Cover, close vent, and cook over low heat until vapor seal is formed (approximately 3-5 minutes.) Continue cooking according to chart. Cooking time begins when vapor seal is formed.

The time guide below is approximate. Actual cooking time will vary on the quantity, age, and size of vegetable being cooked.

Vegetable	Cooking Time *
Artichokes	30-45 minutes
Asparagus	10-15 minutes
Beans, Yellow/Green	20-25 minutes
Beans, Lima	30-35 minutes
Beets, whole	35-40 minutes
Broccoli	15-20 minutes
Brussel Sprouts	15-20 minutes
Cabbage, shredded	10-15 minutes
Carrots, sliced	15-20 minutes
Cauliflower	10-15 minutes
Chinese Pea Pods	3-5 minutes
Corn**	10-12 minutes
Eggplant	5-8 minutes
Greens	10-12 minutes
Leeks	12-15 minutes
Mushrooms	4-5 minutes
Okra	15-20 minutes
Onions, whole	15-20 minutes
Parsnips, sliced	15-20 minutes
Peas	5-7 minutes
Potatoes, White, quartered	20-25 minutes
Potatoes, Sweet	30-35 minutes
Potatoes, baked	30-35 minutes
Spinach	8-10 minutes
Squash, Summer	15-20 minutes
Squash, Winter	25-30 minutes
Tomatoes	10-15 minutes
Turnips, Rutabagas	25-30 minutes

*Cooking time on low after vapor seal is formed.

**For corn on the cob, remove husks and silks, reserving husks. Cover the bottom of the utensil with a double layer of corn husks. Place corn in layers on husks, rinse, pour water off, cover, close vent, and form vapor seal over low heat. Cook 10 to 12 minutes or until tender depending on the size of ears.

PASTA DICTIONARY

Acini di pepe: "Peppercorns"; tiny little solid beads.

Anellini: "Little rings."

Bows: The American version of Italian farfalle, or "butterflies"; often egg noodle dough.

Bucatini: A long round thin spaghetti with a pierced hollow down the center.

Capellini: Means "fine hairs," very delicate round noodles; sometimes called capelli d'angelo, or "angel hair."

Cavatelli: A short curled noodle, available fresh, frozen, and dried; the dried are shell-shaped with a slightly ruffled outside.

Conchigle: See description for 'Shells.'

Conchigliette: "Tiny shells."

Coralli: Tiny tubes; similar to tubettini.

Ditalini: "Little thimbles."

Elbows: Tiny shapes suitable for soups

Farfalle: See description for 'Bows.'

Farfalline: "Tiny butterflies."

Fedelini: Thin spaghetti cut into short curved lengths.

Fusilli: A long fat solid spiral spaghetti, or a short fat screw-like pasta similar to rotella.

Gamelli: Means "twins," because it looks like two short fat pieces of spaghetti twisted together.

Mezzani: A tubular pasta 1 to 2 inches (2.5 to 5 cm) long with a smooth exterior; the same pasta with ridged exterior is called mezzani rigati.

Mostaccioli: Means "small mustaches," cut looks like penne.

Orecchiette: "Little ears," which are round fat little (about ½ inch or 1.5 cm) saucer like disks.

Orzo: Rice shape; also called riso or rosamarina.

Penne: A tubular pasta, about 1½ inches (4 cm) in length; the ends are cut diagonally to resemble a quill or a pen point, smooth exterior or ridged (rigati).

Perciatelli: A fatter version of Bucatini.

Pastina: Very tiny grains of dough; for soup.

Quadrettini: Small flat squares.

Radiatore: A short fat pasta shape rippled and ringed like a radiator.

Rigatoni: Very large grooved tubular pasta.

Riso: Orzo; rosamarina.

Rotella: A short 1½ to 2 inch (4 to 5 cm) fat screw like shape; sometimes called fusilli.

Semi di mela: "Apple seed."

Semi di melone: "Melon seed."

Shells: Available from tiny to jumbo; called conchiglie and maruzze.

Spaghetti: A long and thin solid round strand of pasta.

Spaghettini: Same as spaghetti, but thinner.

Stellini: "Little star."

Tubettini: "Tiny tubes."

Vermecelli: Very thin strands of pasta, often sold in clusters.

Ziti: A large tubular macaroni, slightly curved, called "bridegrooms."

❖　❖　❖　❖　❖

Grains

Cooking Instructions

Bring liquid to boil over medium heat, add grain, stir, cover, and reduce heat to low for required cooking time. Do not restir. Fluff with a fork to separate grains before serving. Grains are also an excellent choice for stack cooking, stack on another utensil after grain has been added.

Grain	Grain : Liquid		Cooking Time	Yield
Amaranth	1 cup : 3 cups	720 ml	25 minutes	2⅔ cups
Barley, Flaked	1 cup : 3 cups	720 ml	15 minutes	3 cups
Barley, Pearled	1 cup : 2 ½ cups	600 ml	30-40 minutes	2½ cups
Buckwheat Groats	1 cup : 2 cups	480 ml	10 minutes	3½ cups
Bulgur	1 cup : 2 cups	480 ml	15 minutes	2½ cups
Cornmeal	1 cup : 4 cups	960 ml	30 minutes	3 cups
Couscous	1 cup : 1⅔ cups	400 ml	5 minutes*	3 cups
Farina	3 tbl : 1 cup	240 ml	½ minute	1 cup
Millet	1 cup : 3 cups	720 ml	20 minutes	4½ cups
Oat Groats	1 cup : 3 cups	720 ml	40 minutes	2½ cups
Oats, Rolled	1 cup : 2 cups	480 ml	15 minutes	4 cups
Oats, Quick	1 cup : 2 cups	480 ml	1 minute	2 cups
Quinoa	1 cup : 2 cups	480 ml	15 minutes	3½ cups
Rice, Brown	1 cup : 2 cups	480 ml	35 minutes	2½ cups
Rice, White	1 cup : 2 cups	480 ml	30 minutes	2½ cups
Rice, Instant	1 cup : 1 cup	240 ml	5 minutes*	2 cups
Rice, Parboiled	¼ cup : ½ cup	120 ml	20 minutes	1 cup
Rice, Wild	1 cup : 4 cups	960 ml	50 minutes	3½ cups
Rye Flakes	1 cup : 2 cups	480 ml	15 minutes	4 cups
Rye Berries	1 cup : 2 cups	480 ml	60 minutes	2½ cups
Soy Grits	1 cup : 1 cup	240 ml	5 minutes*	2 cups
Wheat Berries	1 cup : 2 cups	480 ml	60 minutes	2½ cups
Wheat, Cracked	1 cup : 2½ cups	600 ml	30 minutes	3 cups

* Add hot liquid, cover, remove from heat.

Eggs

Soft Cooked Eggs

In a cool 1-quart saucepan (1.5 L utensil) place eggs and 2 tablespoons water for one egg, adding 1 tablespoon for each additional egg, up to six. (Use ½ cup (120 ml) water for more than 6 eggs.)

Cover pan. Cook on medium heat until steam appears, about 2 minutes.

For electric range turn off heat. For gas range, turn flame to as low as possible. Time eggs from the instant steam appears. Continue cooking 3-4 minutes for soft cooked, 5 minutes for very firm white and medium soft yolk.

Hard Cooked Eggs

Use same method as above, adding additional water for additional eggs.

Cover. Place over medium heat cooking for 5 minutes. Turn burner off and leave covered 10 minutes.

Cool in cold water, then peel.

Poached Eggs

Pour 1 cup (240 ml) hot water into large frypan with grater/steamer tray. Break eggs into lightly buttered egg cups. Place on grater/steamer tray. Cover with 4 L dome cover. Cook over medium heat until steam appears. Reduce to low. Continue cooking 3-4 minutes for soft cooked eggs, or longer to desired firmness.

STAYING FIT WITH HEALTH CRAFT

There is increasing evidence that certain foods may help prevent or hinder some types of cancer. While the evidence continues to accumulate, adding these foods to your diet certainly cannot hurt and likely will help.

It is a particularly smart diet strategy. Eating many kinds of fruits and vegetables is sound advice from the American Cancer Society on cancer-proofing your diet. Most experts also recommend cutting down on fats and eating healthy amounts of fiber — the same prescription that experts say reduces heart attack risks. Maintaining your foods' natural goodness by cooking them properly only makes good sense.

As human beings there are four major factors that influence our health: heredity, the environment, nutrition, and the amount and type of exercise we get.

We have the most control over our nutrition and the amount we exercise. This section has been designed as a primer on nutrition, to help you find a more healthful way to eat. By understanding where we currently are on the road to nutrition, we will all live longer, more healthful lives.

A quote from the Surgeon General's Report on Nutrition & Health focuses on the cultural and social pleasures of our heritage.

"Food sustains us, it can be a source of considerable pleasure, it is a reflection of our rich social fabric and cultural heritage, and it adds valued dimensions to our lives. Yet what we eat may affect our risk for several of the leading causes of death for Americans, notably, coronary heart disease, stroke, atherosclerosis, diabetes, and some types of cancer. These disorders together now account for more than two-thirds of all deaths in the United States."

The report brings to the forefront the dangers associated with the American diet. As this chart illustrates five of the top ten causes of death in the United States are influenced by our diet.

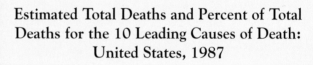

Estimated Total Deaths and Percent of Total Deaths for the 10 Leading Causes of Death: United States, 1987

Rank	Cause of Death	Number	Percent of Total Deaths
1[a]	Heart Diseases	759,400	35.7
	(Coronary heart disease)	(511,700)	(24.1)
	(Other heart disease	(247,700)	(11.6)
2[a]	Cancers	476,700	22.4
3[a]	Strokes	148,700	7.0
4[b]	Unintentional injuries	92,500	4.4
	(Motor vehicle)	(46,800)	(2.2)
	(All others)	(45,700)	(2.2)
5	Chronic obstructive lung diseases	78,000	3.7
6	Pneumonia and influenza	68,600	3.2
7[a]	Diabetes mellitus	37,800	1.8
8[b]	Suicide	29,600	1.4
9[b]	Chronic liver disease and cirrhosis	26,000	1.2
10[a]	Atherosclerosis	23,100	1.1
....	All causes	2,125,100	100.0

[a]Causes of death in which diet plays a part.

[b]Causes of death in which excessive alcohol consumption plays a part.

Source: National Center for Health Statistics, Monthly Vital Statistics Report, vol. 37, no. 1, April 25, 1988.

FOOD GUIDE PYRAMID

The new Food Guide Pyramid from the Food & Drug Administration replaces the basic four food groups we grew up with.

The pyramid takes the original food groups and expands them into the nutritional ingredients required in our daily diets today. A few years ago few of us knew what a complex carbohydrate was, we now are beginning to learn. The same is true for the fats in our diet. The basic four did not have a place for fats or cholesterol, which fell basically into two categories, the meat group and the milk group. We now know, through medical research, that the amount of fats in our diet affects not only our waistlines but our chances of longevity as well. The same is true for the amount of fiber we eat.

This is why this book has been designed with a nutritional breakdown of every recipe, per serving. This information will allow you to plan more healthful as well as delicious meals.

How many servings do you need?
(Guidelines apply to ages 2 and older.)

	Sedentary Women Older Adults	Children, Teenage Girls, Active Women Sedentary Men	Teenage Boys Active Men, Very Active Women
Grains	6	9	11
Vegetables	3	4	5
Fruit	2	3	4
Milk	2-3	2-3	2-3
Meat (ounces)	5	6	7
Fat (grams)	53	73	93

What counts as a serving?

Bread, Cereals, Rice, Pasta

1 slice soft-crust bread (1oz.), ½ English muffin, regular bagel, or soft pretzel, ½ bun or pita (1oz.), ½ slice firm hearth loaf, ½ oz. crackers, cookies or pretzels, ½ medium muffin, 1 small waffle 3½" (9 cm) square, 1 pancake 4" (10 cm), ½ cup cooked rice, bulgur, barley, or other whole grain, ½ cup cooked pasta or couscous, 1 oz cold cereal (amount varies; read labels), ½ cup cooked cereal, (⅓ cup uncooked), 2 cups plain popped popcorn, 1 slice pizza (⅛ of 10" pizza), ½-1 flour or corn tortilla (1oz.)

Vegetables

1 cup raw leafy vegetables, ½ cup cooked or chopped vegetables, ¾ cup juice

Fruit

1 medium apple, banana, orange; ½ cup chopped, cooked, canned; ¾ cup juice

Milk, Yogurt, Cheese

1 cup milk or yogurt, 1½ ounces natural cheese, 2 ounces processed cheese

Meat, Poultry, Fish, Dry Beans, Eggs, Nuts

2-3 oz. lean meat, poultry or fish; ½ cup cooked dry beans, 1 egg, or 2 tablespoons peanut butter count as 1 ounce lean meat

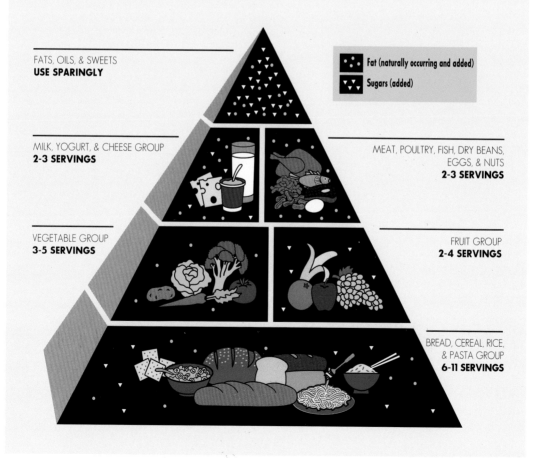

Take Control

How do you make a change and take control of your own health. The American Cancer Society recommends the following:

Reduce Your Risk of Cancer

Make a commitment to yourself today to make healthy food choices. Choose foods high in vitamin A, vitamin C, and fiber and consume more cruciferous vegetables.

Foods high in vitamin A may help protect you against cancers of the esophagus, larynx, and lung. Choose squash, apricot, and spinach. Fresh foods are the best source of beta-carotene not vitamin pills. Likewise, vitamin C may help protect against cancers of the esophagus and stomach and is found naturally in many fresh foods and vegetables. Adding high fiber may protect you against colon cancer and cruciferous vegetables (the cabbage family type) appear to protect against colon, stomach, and respiratory cancers. Many foods are natural multi-sources to reduce your risks of cancers.

TAKE CONTROL

PROTECTIVE FACTORS

1. GREEN VEGETABLES. Eat more of the crucifers: Brussel sprouts, broccoli, cauliflower, all cabbages, and kale.

2. HIGH-FIBER FOODS. Eat more whole grains, fruits and vegetables, wheat and bran cereals, rice, popcorn, and whole-wheat breads.

3. VITAMIN A. Eat foods with beta-carotene: carrots, peaches, apricots, squash, and broccoli.

4. VITAMIN C. Eat fresh fruits and vegetables like grapefruit, cantaloupe, oranges, strawberries, red and green peppers, broccoli, and tomatoes.

5. WEIGHT CONTROL. Control your weight through regular exercise and sensible eating.

RISK FACTORS

6. HIGH-FAT DIET. Cut fat intake. Eat lean meats, fish, skinned poultry and low-fat dairy products. Avoid pastries and candies.

7. SODIUM AND FOOD PRESERVATIVES. Choose these foods only occasionally: Bacon, ham, hot dogs, or salt-cured fish.

8. TOBACCO. Smoking is the biggest cancer risk factor of all. Pick a quit day now.

9. ALCOHOL. Linked to kidney and liver disease. If you drink, do so in moderation.

10. EXCESSIVE SUN. Can cause skin cancer and other damage. Protect yourself with sunscreen.

Why We Cook
- To make food more palatable and appetizing
- To kill harmful bacteria on food
- To make food more digestible
- To entertain, be creative, and have fun

Keep in mind however, a selection of foods has always been available —what we do to them prior to consumption either adds to or subtracts from their nutritional value and to our health.

Dietary Intake
The following chart shows the current percentages of average dietary intake in the United States. As you can see in this country complex carbohydrate consumption is a mere 58 percent of what it should be. The same is true for sugar consumption only reversed. We eat more, not less, sugar than we should, and our fat intake skyrockets.

CURRENT LEVELS

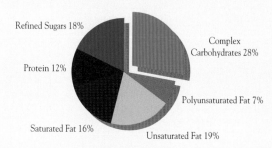

Refined Sugars 18%

Complex Carbohydrates 28%

Protein 12%

Polyunsaturated Fat 7%

Saturated Fat 16%

Unsaturated Fat 19%

RECOMMENDED LEVELS

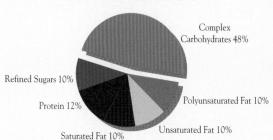

Complex Carbohydrates 48%

Refined Sugars 10%

Protein 12%

Polyunsaturated Fat 10%

Saturated Fat 10%

Unsaturated Fat 10%

Suggestions:
- Eat a variety of foods.
- Maintain desirable weight.
- Avoid too much fat, saturated fat, and cholesterol.
- Eat foods with adequate starch and fiber.
- Avoid too much sugar.
- Avoid too much sodium.
- If you drink alcoholic beverages, do so in moderation.

Basics on Metabolism

Metabolism is the process by which food is converted into useful energy. This begins with chemical processes in the gastrointestinal tract changing plant and animal food into less complex components so that they can be absorbed to fulfill their various functions in the body — growth, repair, and fuel. The body gets this energy in the form of carbohydrates, protein, and fats. We measure the energy available in foods, and the energy needed for metabolism, physical activity and digestion, as kilocalories, kcalories, or commonly known and hereafter referred to as a *calorie*.

Carbohydrates provide 4 calories per gram. Proteins provide 4 calories per gram. Fats provide 9-11 calories per gram. The daily caloric need of individuals varies widely and is dependent on height, weight, age, level of activity, state of health, and probably heredity. It is generally accepted that the "typical" adult woman needs 1,500 to 1,800 calories each day and the "typical" man needs 2,000 to 3,000 calories.

> Carbohydrates provide 4 calories per gram.
>
> Proteins provide 4 calories per gram.
>
> Fats provide over twice as many— 9-11 calories per gram.

Each pound of human body fat has about 3,500 calories of energy. Body fat is converted into energy when the calorie intake in food is inadequate. Likewise, calories eaten in excess of need go into energy reserves as body fat. A pound of body fat can be lost in one week by reducing energy intake by approximately 500 calories per day, or increasing physical activity by 500 calories per day. A combination of decreased intake and increased output leads to the recommended healthy two pounds per week rate of weight loss. The goal should be a slow, healthy weight loss that allows time for the body metabolism and past eating habits to change, and also facilitates permanent weight loss.

Fats are stored in the body and used as a later energy source. The body's metabolism of fat is a very complex process. Some fat must be included in the diet as fat has many important functions in our bodies including insulation, padding, and transportation of fat soluble vitamins which have the following functions:

Vitamin A is essential for vision, cell growth and development, reproduction, a strong immune system, healthy hair, skin, and mucous membranes;

Vitamin D is essential for proper metabolism of calcium to make strong bones and teeth;

Vitamin E is essential for healthy nerve function and reproduction;

Vitamin K is essential for clotting of blood.

Metabolic Facts

Fat calories are preferentially deposited as body fat, whereas carbohydrates are more likely to be burned as body heat, for example — eating 100 calories of pretzels (carbohydrates) results in 25 calories being used for digestion and processing and 75 calories left to be stored; — eating 100 calories of salad dressing (fat) results in 3 to 5 calories being used for digestion with 95 to 97 calories left to be stored.

Fatty acids in the small intestine are passively absorbed, using no calories; carbohydrates and proteins both require calories in their digestive process.

Eating fats with sugar may create increased obesity because sugar stimulates the release of insulin which encourages excessive fat storage.

Extremely low-fat diets (less than 20 percent of total calories in fat) will not necessarily cause weight loss because the individual may eat excessive calories from other sources.

We need to aim for a healthy ratio of body fat and lean muscle mass which is 15 to 20 percent body fat for men and 19 to 24 percent for women.

Muscles need fat as their energy source while performing light or moderate activities including sleep.

In the muscle, fat is only burned for fuel in the presence of oxygen and carbohydrates.

Include regular moderate level aerobic exercise to increase oxidation of stored body fat.

To have adequate nutritional intake and lower fat — have at least five servings of fruits and vegetables a day and exercise 30 minutes five times a week.

Lower Your Fat Intake

Choose lower fat foods using some of the following suggestions:

High Fat Foods	Lower Fat Substitutes
Whole or 2% milk	Skim or ½% milk
Whole milk cheeses	Low-fat cheese, skim milk cheeses
Butter	Reduced-calorie margarine
Lard, meat fat, shortening	Reduced-calorie margarine, vegetable cooking spray
Gravy with meat drippings	Gravy with bouillon or defattened broth
Salad dressing	Lemon, vinegar, reduced-calorie dressings, oil-free or fat-free dressings
4% fat cottage cheese	1% low-fat cottage cheese
Cream cheese	Light cream cheese produce, Neufchatel, fat-free cream cheese
Sour cream	Low-fat sour cream, plain low-fat and non-fat yogurt
Ice cream	Ice milk, low-fat frozen yogurt, sherbet, sorbet
Whole eggs	Egg whites, egg substitutes
Heavily marbled meats	Lean cuts of beef, pork, and poultry
Bacon,sausage	Canadian bacon, lean ham, low-fat sausage
Bologna, salami, pastrami, frankfurters	Sliced turkey or chicken without skin, lean roast beef, lean ham
Oil-packed tuna	Water-packed tuna
Croissants, butter rolls, doughnuts	Bagels, English muffins, matzos, air-popped popcorn
Butter crackers, potato chips, corn chips, etc.	Pretzels, rice cakes, bread sticks, whole grain breads

Understand and Use Food Labels

The new label format should make food shopping much easier for all Americans. It will be especially helpful for those who need to limit certain nutrients due to illness or for disease prevention.

The following is an adaptation of the new label.

The new food label carries an up-to-date easier-to-use nutrition information guide, to be required on almost all packaged foods (compared to about 60 percent of products up until now). The guide serves as a key to help in planning a healthy diet.

1. The new title, Nutrition Facts, signals that the label contains the newly required information.

2. Serving sizes are now more consistent across product lines, stating both household and metric measures, and reflect the amounts people actually eat.

3. Calories from fat are now shown on the label to help consumers meet dietary guidelines that recommend people get no more than 30 percent of their calories from fat.

4. Daily Value shows how a food fits into the overall daily diet for 2,000 calories.

5. The list of nutrients covers those most important to the health of today's consumers, most of whom need to worry about getting too much of certain items (fat, for example) rather than too few vitamins or minerals, as in the past. The food's producer may also add information about other vitamins and minerals. Foods that contain only a few of the nutrients required on the standard label can use a short label format. This is also true of very small packages and cans.

6. Daily values are also something new. Some are maximums, as with fat (65 grams or less); others are minimums, as with carbohydrates (300 grams or more). The daily values on the label are based on a daily diet of 2,000 and 2,500 calories. Individuals should adjust the values to fit their own calorie intake.

7. The label now tells the number of calories per gram of fat, carbohydrate, and protein. These amounts are rounded off.

Of the six items shown in bold print on the labels, four — namely calories, total fat, cholesterol, and sodium —will alert consumers to the items that they should eat in moderation. Saturated fat values are also provided.

Nutrition Facts

Serving Size (31g)
Servings Per Container About 9

Amount Per Serving

Calories 140   Calories from Fat 45

	% Daily Value*
Total Fat 5g	**8**%
Saturated Fat 1g	**4**%
Polyunsaturated Fat 0.5g	
Monounsaturated Fat 1.5g	
Cholesterol 0mg	**0**%
Sodium 170mg	**7**%
Total Carbohydrate 21g	**7**%
Dietary Fiber 4g	**14**%
Sugars 0g	
Protein 3g	

Vitamin A 0%	•	Vitamin C	0%
Calcium 0%	•	Iron	8%
Phosphorus 10%			

* Percent Daily Values are based on a 2,000 calorie diet. Your daily values may be higher or lower depending on your calorie needs:

		Calories:	2,000	2,500
Total Fat	Less than		65g	80g
Sat Fat	Less than		20g	25g
Cholesterol	Less than		300mg	300mg
Sodium	Less than		2,400mg	2,400mg
Total de Carbohydrate			300g	375g
Dietary Fiber			25g	30g

More on Food Labels

Another major advantage of this format is the use of standardized portions for servings. In the past, manufacturers could alter the nutrient content of their products by juggling serving size. For example, in order to make potato chips appear to be low calorie, low fat, and low sodium, the serving size was two chips. The amounts were usually given in ounces or other weights not commonly understood by the public. The new regulations mandate portion sizes that are more typical of the amounts people actually eat. They are also presented in common measurements.

Daily Values (DV) and Percent Daily Values will provide another nutritional content indicator. The Daily Values are the reference numbers set by the government and are based on current nutritional recommendations. These are usually correlated with the 2,000 and 2,500 calorie reference diets on the bottom of the label. The Daily Values for cholesterol, sodium, and potassium are set at a constant amount regardless of calorie level.

The Percent Daily Value (%DV) gives a general idea on the food's nutrient contributions to the 2,000 calorie reference diet. In all cases you must remember that you may need more or less than 2,000 calories per day.

In order to build a healthful diet using these concepts and different calorie levels, use the chart below to find the nutrient amounts and total Percentage Daily Value that are indicated for your calorie level. This will help you compare foods and make informed food choices.

Food Component DV for all Calorie Levels	
Cholesterol	300 mg
Sodium	2,400 mg
Potassium*	3,500 mg
*Optional on Nutrition label	

Guidelines for Percentage Daily Values	
Food Component	Calculated as*
Total fat	30% of total calories
Saturated fat	10% of total calories
Total Carbohydrate	60% of total calories
Dietary Fiber	11.5 gm/1000 calories
Protein**	10% of total calories
* Numbers may be rounded for labeling	
** % Daily Values for protein is optional	

Daily Nutrient Needs for Different Calorie Levels*						
Food Component	1,600	2,000 **	2,200	2,500	2,800	3,200
Total Fat (g)	53	65	73	80	93	107
Saturated Fat (g)	18	20	24	25	31	36
Total Carbohydrate	240	300	330	375	420	480
Dietary Fiber (g)	20 ***	25	25	30	32	37
Protein	46 ****	50	55	64	70	80

Your total % Daily Value for each of these nutrients in all the foods you eat in one day can add up to:

	80%	100%	110%	125%	140%	160%

*Numbers may be rounded.
**%Daily Value on the label for total fat, saturated fat, carbohydrate, dietary fiber, and protein (if listed is based on a 2,000 calorie reference diet.)
***20 g is the minimum amount of fiber recommended for all calorie levels below 1,800. Source: National Cancer Institute.
****46g is the minimum amount of protein recommended for all calorie levels below 1,800. Source: Recommended Dietary Allowances, 1989.
NOTE: These calorie levels may not apply to children and adolescents who have varying caloric requirements. For specific advice concerning calorie levels, please consult a registered dietitian, qualified health professional, or pediatrician.

Another positive aspect of the new labeling legislation is that it eliminated the use of nutrient content claims that were not valid. The new label format mandates criteria for definition for food claims such as "fat free, high fiber, low calorie" etc.

It is anticipated that new definitions will be developed as manufacturers identify other nutrients needing clarifications.

An area of considerable

Label Claim	Definitions
Calorie free	less than 5 calories
Low calorie	40 calories or less
Light or Lite	⅓ fewer calories or 50% less fat
Light in sodium	50% less sodium
Fat free	Less than ½ gm fat
Low fat	3 grams or less fat
Cholesterol free	less than 2 mg cholesterol and 2 gm or less saturated fat
Low cholesterol	20 mg or less cholesterol and 2 mg or less saturated fat
Sodium free	less than 5 mg sodium
Very low sodium	35 mg or less
Low sodium	140 mg or less
High fiber	5 gm or more

controversy has developed regarding the use of health claims on food packaging. A health claim is defined as a label statement that describes the relationship between a nutrient and a disease or health-related condition. The food must meet specified nutrient levels if it is allowed to make a health claim. Currently, seven types of health claims are allowed.

Nutrient-Disease Relationship
Diet high in calcium reduces risks of osteoporosis
Diet high in fiber-containing grains, fruits, and vegetables reduces risks of cancer
Diet high in fruits or vegetables that are high dietary fiber or vitamin A or C reduces risks of cancer
Diet high in fiber from fruits, vegetables, and grain products reduces risks of heart disease
Diet low in fat reduces risks cancer
Diet low in saturated fat and cholesterol reduces risk of heart disease
Diet low in sodium reduces risk of high blood pressure

New food labels are required on all canned and packaged foods except:

• Foods produced by companies with food sales of less than $50,000 per year
• Restaurant food
• Food prepared for immediate consumption, such as airplane meals
• Ready to eat food prepared mainly on site, such as bakery items
• Food sold by food service vendors
• Food sold in bulk bins
• Plain coffee, tea, spices, and other foods without significant amounts of any nutrients

There is a great deal of excellent label information available to the general public through organizations such as the National Food Processors Association, The American Diabetics Association and the manufacturers of the individual products. As with most things in our lives, the more you know about labels the more freedom you will have in developing healthful meals.

The Point System

Calorie Points are a simplified way of counting calories. This system works for people who want to lose, maintain or gain weight. Many diabetics use it to assist them in the management of their disease.

Calorie points may be used to count several nutrients in addition to calories. The nutrients include, but are not limited to sodium, carbohydrate, fiber, protein, and potassium. Using points makes it easy to manage eating.

The more traditional method of counting calories is time consuming, and not as accurate as most people think. Calorie values published in different books vary as does the caloric content of foods. There may be many calorie differences in the same size apples growing on opposite sides of the same tree. Although counting calories is not exact, the lists of nutrients are the best tool available.

The food lists in currently accepted sources provide the nutrient values used by people who count calories. They are the basis for calorie points. These same lists provide the basis for many other nutrients used in the point system.

Definitions of Points

The nutrients considered have assigned point values as follows:

A Calorie Point is 75 calories abbreviated as (CAL)
A Carbohydrate Point is 15 grams of Carbohydrate abbreviated as (CHO)
A Fiber Point is 2 grams of Dietary Fiber abbreviated as (FIB)
A Sodium Point is 23 milligrams of Sodium abbreviated as (NA)
A Cholesterol Point is 10 milligrams of cholesterol abbreviated as (CHOL)
A Protein Point is 8 grams of Protein abbreviated as (PRO)

The recipes listed and analyzed for Vita Craft provide both nutrient values and points for the six selected nutrients. Counting 20 calorie points instead of 1,500 calories is one example of the simplicity of the calorie point system.

Calorie/Carbohydrate Point Conversions

The first two columns of this table list calories and their conversion values in points. Remember, a calorie point is equal to about 75 calories. The third column is the grams of carbohydrate we suggest for each calorie level and their conversion to carbohydrate points shown in the fourth column. The final columns represent fat calories and grams. It is now easier to count fat as grams because that value is found on all labels. Example: For a 1,500 calorie plan you would want to consume 20 calorie points, 11 carbohydrate points, and 42 grams of fat.

Calories	Points	Grams of Carbohydrate 55% of Total Calories	Carbohydrate Points	Fat 25% of Total Calories	Fat Grams
1,200	16	660	9	300	33
1,300	17 ½	715	9 ½	325	36
1,400	18 ½	770	10	350	39
1,500	20	825	11	375	42
1,600	21 ½	880	12	400	44
1,700	22 ½	935	12 ½	425	47
1,800	24	990	13	450	50
1,900	25 ½	1,045	14	475	53
2,000	26 ½	1,100	14 ½	500	56
2,100	28	1,155	15	525	58
2,200	29 ½	1,210	16	550	61
2,300	31	1,265	17	575	64
2,400	32	1,320	17½	600	67
2,500	33 ½	1,375	18	625	69
2,600	35	1,430	19	650	72
2,700	36	1,485	20	675	75
2,800	37 ½	1,540	20 ½	700	78
2,900	38 ½	1,595	21	725	81
3,000	40	1,650	22	750	83
4,000	53	2,200	29	1,000	111
5,000	67	2,750	36 ½	1,250	139

Fiber Points

Because of the health benefits of including dietary fiber in your diet, we suggest that you count dietary fiber points also. Ten (10) fiber points per day are recommended for the first two-week period. Fifteen (15) fiber points per day are recommended for the second two weeks. Increase to a maximum of 20-25 fiber points per day, as tolerated.

The Issue of Control

A truly successful eating plan is one that is safe, healthy, and allows you to eat the foods you enjoy. You must stay on the new plan until you have modified your harmful behaviors and gained control over eating. The plan is a success when you reach your goal and maintain that new weight. It is best to think of this activity as learning to eat properly rather than being on a diet.

Nine Points to Assist in Control

1. Do not adopt a plan so low in calories that you can't get the needed nutrients and your body slows down leading to decreased calorie burn. A rule of thumb is at least 1,200 calories for females and 1,500 for males.
    A dietitian or your doctor can compute the calorie level that will allow you to lose weight safely. (Factors such as repeated dieting may result in a reduced metabolic rate requiring fewer calories than indicated on the following chart).

Find your weight range and activity level. Multiply your actual weight by the calories per pound shown under your activity level.

CALORIES PER POUND

Weight If Overweight	Sedentary Activity	Light to Moderate Activity	Very Active
up to 200	12	13	15
201 to 250	10	11	12-13
251 to 300	9	10	11
300 and over	8	9	10
If normal weight	12	14	16-18

SEDENTARY ACTIVITY – Most of the day is spent in activities such as TV, reading, handwork, etc.

LIGHT TO MODERATE ACTIVITY – Most of the day is spent in activities such as walking, housework, golf, etc.

VERY ACTIVE – Most of the day is spent in activities such as walking briskly, yard work, scrubbing floors, dancing, etc. A regular exercise program is scheduled.

2. Eat at least three meals and a snack if desired. These must be within the allowed calories and fat grams. This plan keeps you from getting too hungry and, therefore, out of control.

3.   Do not weigh yourself more than once a week. Remember that a 1-2 pound loss per week or 4-10 pounds per month will be the most healthful and permanent loss.

4.   Take the time to identify current bad habits and create ways to overcome them.

5.   Write down the foods eaten and point values for the nutrients you are counting. Writing the items down is the only way to keep track of intake for the first few months.

6.   Exercise daily to improve your calorie burn, muscle tone, body configuration, raise your metabolic rate, improve your mental attitude, and relieve stress. The best exercise is aerobic. Two excellent aerobic activities are walking and biking. Start out gradually and work up to at least 30 minutes per session.

7.   Don't let a binge become an excuse to quit. Start on the eating plan again.

8.   Special occasions and foods can be worked into your eating plan.

9.   It is essential that you have a well balanced, adequate nutrient intake. Refer to information on the Food Guide Pyramid on pages 17 and 18 for your basic nutritional needs.

CALORIE, CARBOHYDRATE & SODIUM CONVERSION CHART

The following charts are provided to help you determine points from label information.

Calorie Conversion Chart

Calorie Content On Label	Calorie Point
19-56	½
57-94	1
95-131	1 ½
132-169	2
170-206	2 ½
207-244	3
245-281	3 ½
282-319	4
320-356	4 ½
357-394	5
395-431	5 ½
432-469	6
470-506	6 ½
507-544	7
545-581	7 ½
582-619	8
620-656	8 ½
657-694	9
695-731	9 ½
732-769	10
770-806	10 ½
807-844	11

Carbohydrate Conversion Chart

Carbohydrate Content On Label	Carbohydrate Points
4-11	½
12-19	1
20-26	1 ½
27-34	2
35-41	2 ½
42-49	3
50-56	3 ½
57-64	4
65-71	4 ½
72-79	5
80-86	5 ½
87-94	6
95-101	6 ½
102-109	7
110-116	7 ½
117-124	8
125-131	8 ½
132-139	9
140-146	9 ½
147-154	10

Sodium Conversion Chart

Sodium Content On Label	Sodium Points
13-33	1
34-56	2
57-79	3
80-102	4
103-125	5
126-148	6
149-171	7
172-194	8
195-217	9
218-240	10
333-355	15
448-480	20
563-595	25
678-710	30

Sample Menu for 1500 Calories

A sample menu has been included to help give you ideas for planning. This example includes a cookie to show you that all "fun" foods do not become things of the past. People with more strict needs would have to modify this sample.

		20 Calorie Pts.	11 Carbohy. Pt.	10-20 Fiber Pts.	42 Fat Grams
Breakfast					
cornflakes	1 cup	1.5	1.5	1.5	0
banana	½	1	1	1	0
whole wheat toast	1 slice	1	1	1	1
margarine	1 teaspoon	.5	0	0	5
milk, ½%	1½ cups	1.5	1.5	0	0
Lunch					
whole wheat bread	2 slices	2	2	2	2.5
turkey	2 ounces	1	0	0	7.5
cheese	¾ ounce	1	0	0	1
salad dressing	½ tablespoon	.5	0	0	1
carrot sticks	6-8 sticks	0	0	.5	0
oatmeal chocolate chip cookie	1	1	.5	1	2.5
Snack					
whole wheat crackers	2	1	1	1	0
peanut butter	1 tablespoon	1.5	.5	.5	2.5
Dinner					
lean roast beef	2 ounces	2	0	0	10
baked potato	1	2	2	2	0
margarine	2 teaspoons	1	0	0	10
green beans	½ cup	0	0	1	0
spinach salad	½ cup	0	0	2.5	0
dressing	1 tablespoon	1	0	0	0
strawberries	¾ cup	.5	.5	1	0
whipped topping	1 tablespoon	0	0	0	0
		20	11.5	15	43

Appetizers
Soups ❖ Salads

Chickpea Soup with Cumin and Cilantro

Sopa de Garbanzas

Serves: 6
Preparation Time: 40 minutes

1½ cups cooked chickpeas
1   onion, coarsely chopped
1½ teaspoons cumin seeds, ground
4   cups (1 L) low sodium beef or chicken stock
1   tablespoon flour
3   tablespoons butter
½   cup (120 ml) light cream,* or half and half (optional)
    salt and pepper to taste
2   tablespoons cilantro, chopped

In 3-quart saucepan (3 L utensil) combine chickpeas, onion, cumin, and stock. Bring to a boil. Reduce heat and simmer for 20 minutes. Puree the mixture in a food mill or blender and return it to the pan.

In separate bowl, make a paste by mixing the flour and 2 tablespoons of the butter and add to the soup in small pinches. After each addition, whisk until smooth. Simmer the soup for 10 minutes.

Add the remaining 1 tablespoon butter and cream while stirring. Add salt and pepper to taste. Serve in individual bowls and garnish with cilantro.

* To reduce fat, omit cream (cream is included in nutritional breakdown).

NUTRITIONAL BREAKDOWN
PER SERVING

Calories 220
Fat Grams 14
Carbohydrate Grams 17
Protein Grams 7
Cholesterol mg 25
Sodium mg 266
THE POINT SYSTEM
Calorie Points 3
Protein Points 1
Fat Grams 14
Sodium Points 12
Fiber Points 2
Carbohydrate Points 1
Cholesterol Points 3

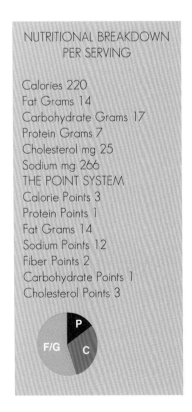

1	10 ½ ounce (300 g) can mandarin orange
1	8 ounce (230 g) can pineapple tidbits or
½	fresh pineapple, cubed
1½	cups small strawberries or
	seedless red grapes
1	medium apple
½	cup pineapple yogurt
½	teaspoon poppy seeds
	lettuce leaves

Poppy Seed Fruit Salad

Serves: 5
Preparation Time: 15 minutes

Drain mandarin oranges; drain pineapple, reserving 1 tablespoon juice. If using strawberries, cut them in half. Core apple and cut into bite-size pieces. Mix all fruit in a medium bowl. Toss lightly to mix. For dressing, in a small mixing bowl stir together yogurt, poppy seeds and the reserved pineapple juice. To serve, line salad plates with the lettuce leaves. Arrange fruit mixture on lettuce. Drizzle dressing over fruit.

NUTRITIONAL BREAKDOWN
PER SERVING

Calories 101
Fat Grams 1
Carbohydrate Grams 23
Protein Grams 2
Cholesterol mg 1
Sodium mg 16
THE POINT SYSTEM
Calorie Points 1½
Protein Points 0
Fat Grams 1
Sodium Points 1/2
Fiber Points 1
Carbohydrate Points 1½
Cholesterol Points 0

Thai Grilled Sirloin Salad

Serves: 8
Preparation Time: 45 minutes

1	teaspoon pepper, freshly ground
1	pound (460 g) beef sirloin, trimmed
½	head red cabbage, shredded
1	head romaine lettuce, cut in 1" (2.5 cm) strips
½	cup mint leaves
2	shallots, thinly sliced and separated into rings
8	green onions, chopped including tops
2	hot peppers, seeded and finely chopped
1	can chicken broth
1	teaspoon fresh lime juice
2	tablespoons fish sauce
1	teaspoon sugar
1	teaspoon roasted rice powder*

*See recipe for roasted rice powder in the Spice section on page 201.

Preheat large frypan over medium-high heat. Rub black pepper into meat. Sear meat in frypan, turning when it releases itself, leave on second side 3 minutes only. You want the beef very rare. Remove to platter and place in freezer 30 minutes to 4 hours.

While meat is cooling, combine cabbage, romaine lettuce, mint leaves, shallots, green onions and hot peppers.

Slice meat very thin across the grain. In same frypan (drain any fat) combine chicken broth, lime juice, fish sauce, sugar and rice powder. Bring to a boil. When boiling add sliced beef and immediately remove from heat. Pour over prepared salad and toss well. Serve with soy sauce if desired.

NUTRITIONAL BREAKDOWN PER SERVING:

Calories 113
Fat Grams 3
Carbohydrate Grams 8
Protein Grams 13
Cholesterol mg 44
Sodium mg 469
THE POINT SYSTEM
Calorie Points 1½
Protein Points 2
Fat Grams 3
Sodium Points 20
Fiber Points 1
Carbohydrate Points ½
Cholesterol Points 4

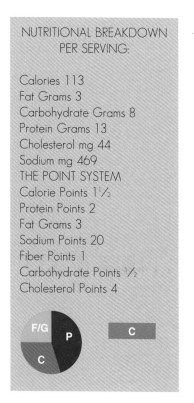

2	strips bacon, sliced
5	white potatoes, sliced
1	onion diced
¼	cup (60 ml) vinegar
2	tablespoons sugar

German Potato Salad

Serves: 6-8 ❖ Yields: 4 cups
Preparation Time: 30 minutes

In the large frypan over medium heat brown bacon pieces. Remove from frypan with slotted spoon. Add potatoes and onion, cover, reduce to medium-low heat for 20 minutes, stirring occasionally to turn potatoes. Mix vinegar and sugar, pour over potatoes, return bacon pieces to frypan and mix.

Serve as a side dish with sausages or ribs.

NUTRITIONAL BREAKDOWN
PER SERVING:

Calories 168
Fat Grams 2
Carbohydrate Grams 34
Protein Grams 4
Cholesterol mg 3
Sodium mg 71
THE POINT SYSTEM
Calorie Points 2
Protein Points 0
Fat Grams 2
Sodium Points 3
Fiber Points 1
Carbohydrate Points 2½
Cholesterol Points 0

Orange Cucumber Salad

Serves: 4
Preparation Time: 10 minutes

½	large cucumber, thinly sliced
¼	teaspoon salt
	dash pepper
1	11 ounce (310 g) can mandarin orange sections, drained
½	cup green pepper, chopped
2	tablespoons parsley, snipped
½	cup plain yogurt
¼	teaspoon ground thyme
	salad greens

In small mixing bowl, sprinkle cucumber with the salt and pepper; toss with orange sections, green pepper, and parsley. In separate bowl combine yogurt and thyme; spoon onto salad mixture. Toss lightly to coat. Cover and chill.

Serve on crisp salad greens.

NUTRITIONAL BREAKDOWN
PER SERVING:

Calories 46
Fat Grams 0
Carbohydrate Grams 9
Protein Grams 3
Cholesterol mg 1
Sodium mg 157
THE POINT SYSTEM
Calorie Points ½
Protein Points ½
Fat Grams 0
Sodium Points 7
Fiber Points ½
Carbohydrate Points ½
Cholesterol Points 0

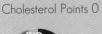

MEATBALLS

½   pound (230 g) extra lean ground beef
1   teaspoon of fresh basil
2   cloves garlic, minced
¼   cup (60 ml) tomato juice from concentrate
1   tablespoon of ketchup
½   cup bread crumbs
1   egg
    salt and pepper to taste

SOUP

3   14.5 ounce (410 g) cans low sodium chicken broth
2   cups (480 ml) water
3   eggs, beaten
1   cup pastina pasta
4   cups whole fresh spinach leaves

Mix together ingredients for meatballs and shape into small balls. Brown in small frypan over medium heat. Remove with slotted spoon to paper towels to drain.

In 3-quart saucepan (3 L utensil), mix together broth and water. Bring to a boil, then swirl in beaten eggs.

Place 3-4 meatballs in a bowl. Add two spinach leaves and 1 tablespoon pastina pasta to each bowl. Pour broth mixture over top to serve.

Wedding Soup

Serves: 8
Preparation Time: 40 minutes

NUTRITIONAL BREAKDOWN
PER SERVING:

Calories 167
Fat Grams 8
Carbohydrate Grams 12
Protein Grams 12
Cholesterol mg 130
Sodium mg 230
THE POINT SYSTEM
Calorie Points 2
Protein Points 2
Fat Grams 8
Sodium Points 10
Fiber Points ½
Carbohydrate Points 1
Cholesterol Points 13

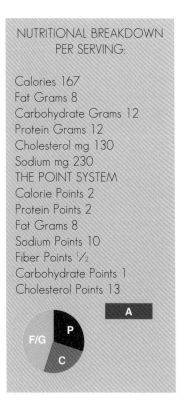

Chinese Salad

2	tablespoons butter
2	3 ounce (85 g) packages Ramen noodles, crushed
¼	cup sliced almonds
1	tablespoon sesame seeds
¼	cup (60 ml) vinegar
½	cup sugar
¼	cup (60 ml) oil
2	tablespoons low sodium soy sauce
1	head Napa cabbage, chopped
1	bunch green onions, chopped

Serves: 10
Preparation Time: 20-30 minutes

In 10" chef pan or large frypan melt butter over medium heat. Add Ramen noodles, almonds, and sesame seeds. Brown slowly. Set aside and allow to cool completely.

Meanwhile, mix vinegar, sugar, oil and soy sauce in 1-quart saucepan (1.5 L utensil). Bring to a boil over medium heat, boil 2 minutes, remove from heat and set aside. Chop cabbage and onions, place in salad bowl. Add cooled Ramen mixture and dressing. Toss well and serve immediately.

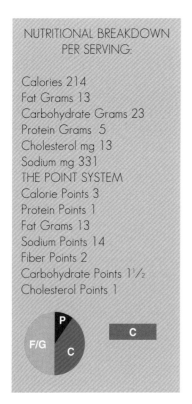

NUTRITIONAL BREAKDOWN
PER SERVING:

Calories 214
Fat Grams 13
Carbohydrate Grams 23
Protein Grams 5
Cholesterol mg 13
Sodium mg 331
THE POINT SYSTEM
Calorie Points 3
Protein Points 1
Fat Grams 13
Sodium Points 14
Fiber Points 2
Carbohydrate Points 1½
Cholesterol Points 1

Layer Salad

1	head lettuce of choice washed and spun dry, torn in bite-size pieces
1	8 ounce (230 g) package frozen peas
½	red onion, sliced thin
3	teaspoons sugar
1	8 ounce (230 g) package Swiss cheese, shredded
½	cup nonfat yogurt
¼	cup nonfat mayonnaise

Serves: 10
Preparation Time: 30 minutes

In salad bowl layer prepared ingredients in 3 layers; first a layer of lettuce, then one-third portion of onions spread evenly over the greens, sprinkle 1 teaspoon sugar over onions, add one-third portion of peas and one-third portion of the Swiss cheese. Repeat layers twice more. Combine yogurt and mayonnaise and spread evenly over top.

Salad may be kept at this point for 24 hours before serving. To serve, toss well to blend ingredients.

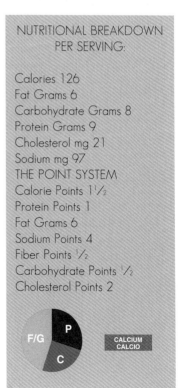

NUTRITIONAL BREAKDOWN
PER SERVING:

Calories 126
Fat Grams 6
Carbohydrate Grams 8
Protein Grams 9
Cholesterol mg 21
Sodium mg 97
THE POINT SYSTEM
Calorie Points 1½
Protein Points 1
Fat Grams 6
Sodium Points 4
Fiber Points ½
Carbohydrate Points ½
Cholesterol Points 2

F/G P C

CALCIUM
CALCIO

Chinese Beef-Noodle Soup

Serves: 12
Preparation Time: 2½ hours

2½	pounds (1.2 kg) beef short ribs
7	cups (1.7 L) water
¼	cup (60 ml) low sodium soy sauce
¼	cup (60 ml) dry sherry
1	tablespoon sugar
6	slices fresh ginger, ¼" (75 mm) thick
8	green onions, chopped
4	cloves garlic, chopped
1	teaspoon aniseed
¼	teaspoon dried hot red pepper flakes
2	turnips, peeled and cut into ¾" (2 cm) cubes
6	ounces (180 g) egg noodles or rice noodles

In 6-quart saucepan (6 L utensil) combine ribs, water, soy sauce, sherry, and sugar. Bring to boil, skim off froth. Add ginger, half of green onions, garlic, aniseed, and pepper flakes. Reduce heat, cover and simmer two hours.

Remove from heat. Cool 30 minutes. Remove ribs with slotted spoon. Chop meat, discarding fat and bones. Strain broth through fine sieve into large saucepan. Add chopped meat. Skim fat or—if time permits—refrigerate and lift fat from surface. Add turnips to broth, simmer covered 10 minutes, add noodles, simmer 7 minutes or until done. Serve with chopped green onions.

NUTRITIONAL BREAKDOWN
PER SERVING

Calories 234
Fat Grams 6
Carbohydrate Grams 7
Protein Grams 23
Cholesterol mg 59
Sodium mg 256
THE POINT SYSTEM
Calorie Points 3
Protein Points 3
Fat Grams 6
Sodium Points 11
Fiber Points 0
Carbohydrate Points ½
Cholesterol Points 6

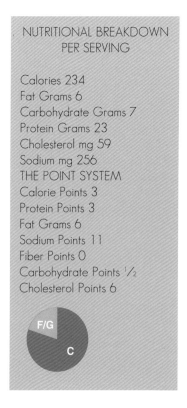

8	onions (Vidalia)
6	cloves garlic
1	tablespoon butter
1	tablespoon oil
3	14.5 ounce (410 g) cans chicken broth
½	cup (120 ml) burgundy wine
6	slices of French bread, ¾" (2 cm) thick
1	cup Monterey Jack, mozzarella or Swiss cheese

In 3-quart saucepan (3 L utensil), over medium heat, caramelize onions and garlic in butter and oil until transparent and creamy, approximately 30 minutes. Add chicken broth and burgundy wine. Simmer covered an additional 30 minutes. Meanwhile, toast French bread in oven until light brown and dry. Ladle soup into broil safe bowls. Place one slice bread on top, cover with mixed cheese. Broil until cheese melts and begins to brown.

French Onion Soup

Serves: 6
Preparation Time: 1 hour, 15 minutes

NUTRITIONAL BREAKDOWN
PER SERVING

Calories 377
Fat Grams 15
Carbohydrate Grams 42
Protein Grams 18
Cholesterol mg 30
Sodium mg 432
THE POINT SYSTEM
Calorie Points 5
Protein Points 2
Fat Grams 15
Sodium Points 19
Fiber Points 2
Carbohydrate Points 3
Cholesterol Points 3

Pinto Bean Soup

Serves: 12
Preparation Time: 1 hour, 30 minutes

❖   ❖   ❖

1	pound (460 g) dried pinto beans
3	medium onions, chopped fine
5	cloves garlic, minced
1	tablespoon olive oil
2	red bell peppers, chopped
1	tablespoon chili powder
2	teaspoons ground cumin
6	cups (1.5 L) water
½	pound (230 g) chorizo (optional)
1	32 ounce (920 g) can tomatoes, chopped
2	cups (480 ml) de-fatted chicken broth
2	tablespoons tomato paste
12	teaspoons fresh lime juice, divided
⅓	cup cilantro, chopped

Rinse and pick over beans. Soak overnight in 2" (5 cm) water (or rinse beans, cover with water, bring to boil 2 minutes, remove from heat and let soak 1 hour).

In 6-quart (6 L) roaster sauté onions and garlic in olive oil until softened. Add red peppers, chili powder and cumin. Drain soaked beans and add to pan with 6 cups (1.5 L) water. Cover, reduce to low heat one hour. If using chorizo, brown and drain on paper towels. Add chorizo, tomatoes, chicken broth and tomato paste to soup, simmer an additional 20 minutes or until heated through.

Serve with 1 teaspoon lime juice in individual bowls. Add chopped cilantro on top.

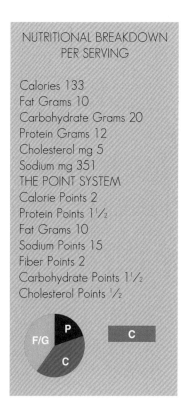

NUTRITIONAL BREAKDOWN
PER SERVING

Calories 133
Fat Grams 10
Carbohydrate Grams 20
Protein Grams 12
Cholesterol mg 5
Sodium mg 351
THE POINT SYSTEM
Calorie Points 2
Protein Points 1½
Fat Grams 10
Sodium Points 15
Fiber Points 2
Carbohydrate Points 1½
Cholesterol Points ½

Roasted Pepper Salad

6   red peppers, cut in half
6   tablespoons (90 ml) olive oil
2   tablespoons red wine vinegar
    salt and pepper
1   clove garlic, chopped
1   green onion, sliced

Serves: 12
Preparation Time: 20 minutes

Flatten red pepper halves with masher or palm of your hand. Preheat large frypan over medium high heat. Brush skin of peppers with oil. Place skin side down in hot frypan, occasionally pressing peppers flat with masher to char skin. Do not turn peppers, cook until skin blackens. Remove from pan and wrap in clean towel to cool for 15-20 minutes. Remove from towel. Using a small knife, peel away the skin. Cut peeled peppers into strips. Mix remaining oil with vinegar, salt and pepper. Place the peppers in serving dish and cover with dressing. Top with green onions and garlic.

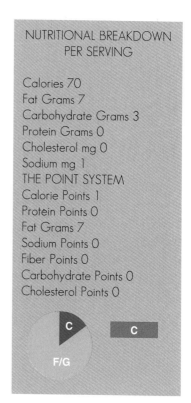

NUTRITIONAL BREAKDOWN
PER SERVING

Calories 70
Fat Grams 7
Carbohydrate Grams 3
Protein Grams 0
Cholesterol mg 0
Sodium mg 1
THE POINT SYSTEM
Calorie Points 1
Protein Points 0
Fat Grams 7
Sodium Points 0
Fiber Points 0
Carbohydrate Points 0
Cholesterol Points 0

Leeks, Mushroom and Potato Soup

Serves: 12-1 cup servings
Preparation Time: 40 minutes

❖   ❖   ❖

3	cups leeks rinsed well, thinly sliced
2	cups fresh mushrooms, thinly sliced
4	cups potatoes, diced
4¼	cups (1.1 L) water
1	cup celery, sliced
1½	teaspoons dry crushed tarragon
1	tablespoon lemon juice
2	teaspoons low-sodium Worcestershire sauce
½	teaspoon ground white pepper
3	tablespoons fresh chives or green onion, minced

Place 4-quart saucepan (4 L utensil) over medium-high heat until hot. Add leeks and mushrooms; cover, cook over medium heat 10 minutes or until tender, stirring twice. Add potatoes, water, and celery. Bring to a boil; cover, reduce heat, and simmer 25 minutes or until potatoes are tender.

Place 1 cup vegetable mixture in blender to purée. Return purée to soup. Stir in tarragon, lemon juice, Worcestershire sauce, and white pepper. Cook until thoroughly heated. Ladle soup into individual bowls, and sprinkle evenly with chives or green onions.

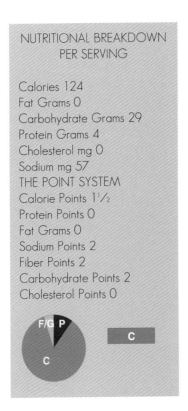

NUTRITIONAL BREAKDOWN
PER SERVING

Calories 124
Fat Grams 0
Carbohydrate Grams 29
Protein Grams 4
Cholesterol mg 0
Sodium mg 57
THE POINT SYSTEM
Calorie Points 1½
Protein Points 0
Fat Grams 0
Sodium Points 2
Fiber Points 2
Carbohydrate Points 2
Cholesterol Points 0

1	head cauliflower
8	green onions
2	teaspoons black mustard seeds
2	teaspoons cumin seeds
1	teaspoon fennel seeds
½	teaspoon turmeric
⅓	cup (80 ml) warm water
¼	cup (60 ml) vegetable oil
⅓	cup fresh cilantro, chopped
1	head romaine lettuce, washed, spun and torn

Indian Cauliflower Salad

Serves: 8
Preparation Time: 20 minutes

Separate cauliflower into 1" (2.5 cm) florets. Peel stems and cut into thin slices. Set aside. Trim onions and chop entire onion including tops. Set aside. Have spices and water ready right next to stove. Heat oil in wok or large frypan over medium-high heat. Add mustard seeds, cumin seeds and fennel seeds. Reduce heat to low. Keep lid handy if seeds sputter too much. When seeds stop sputtering add turmeric and stir, add cauliflower and stir to coat, add water and cover 10 minutes. Place prepared romaine in bowl, top with green onion and cilantro, pour cauliflower over top and toss.

This dish is bright, attractive, unusual, and very good.

Serve with prepared brown rice or low fat sausage.

Caesar Salad and Grilled Chicken

Serves: 4
Preparation Time: 20 minutes

2   chicken breasts, boned and skinned
½   cup non-fat plain yogurt
1   teaspoon anchovy paste
1   teaspoon fresh lime juice
1   teaspoon balsamic vinegar
1   teaspoon Dijon mustard
½   teaspoon Worcestershire sauce
1   clove garlic, minced
¼   cup Parmesan cheese, freshly grated
1   head romaine lettuce, rinsed, spun dry and cut into 1" (2.5 cm) wide strips
½   red onion, sliced very thin
½   red pepper, sliced very thin in rings

Preheat 10" chef pan or large frypan over medium heat until water "dances" on pan. Add chicken breasts, cover, and cook 5 minutes. Turn chicken, cover and cook additional 5 minutes. Remove from pan, shred and place in refrigerator to cool.

For dressing blend together yogurt, anchovy paste, lime juice, balsamic vinegar, Dijon mustard, Worcestershire sauce, garlic, and Parmesan. Place in refrigerator to cool.

To serve: In large bowl add cut romaine, red onion, red pepper, shredded chicken and then dressing. Toss well, top with fresh cracked pepper and salt (optional).

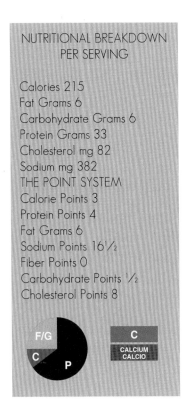

NUTRITIONAL BREAKDOWN
PER SERVING

Calories 215
Fat Grams 6
Carbohydrate Grams 6
Protein Grams 33
Cholesterol mg 82
Sodium mg 382
THE POINT SYSTEM
Calorie Points 3
Protein Points 4
Fat Grams 6
Sodium Points 16½
Fiber Points 0
Carbohydrate Points ½
Cholesterol Points 8

1 cup low calorie mayonnaise
½ tube (1.6 ounce or 45 g) anchovy paste
1 cup low-fat yogurt
1 small can small shrimp, drained
1 small can mushroom pieces
1 clove garlic, minced
2 tablespoons onion, minced
1 tablespoon parsley, chopped

Shrimp Dressing

Yields: 2 cups ❖ Serves: 10
Preparation Time: 10 minutes (8 hours)

Mix all listed ingredients together and let stand 8 hours in refrigerator for flavors to blend thoroughly. Will keep in the refrigerator 10 days. Serve over lettuce with Homemade Croutons, page 59. Shown with optional steamed shrimp.

NUTRITIONAL BREAKDOWN
PER SERVING:

Calories 108
Fat Grams 7
Carbohydrate Grams 4
Protein Grams 7
Cholesterol mg 25
Sodium mg 182
THE POINT SYSTEM
Calorie Points 1½
Protein Points 1
Fat Grams 7
Sodium Points 8
Fiber Points ½
Carbohydrate Points ½
Cholesterol Points 2½

Patata-
Piccata Salad

Serves: 6
Preparation Time: 2 hours

1	pound (460 g) small new potatoes
¼	cup (60 ml) Chablis or other dry white wine
3	tablespoons chicken broth
2	tablespoons water
1	tablespoon olive oil
2	teaspoons tarragon vinegar
2	teaspoons freshly squeezed lemon juice
¼	teaspoon salt
¼	teaspoon fresh ground black pepper
2	tablespoons sugar
3	tablespoons green onions, minced
3	tablespoons fresh parsley, minced
1	tablespoon capers, chopped

Wash and dry potatoes. Cook in small frypan over medium heat covered 45 minutes until tender; cool slightly. Cube potatoes, and place in a medium bowl. Add wine; toss gently. Let stand 15 minutes, tossing occasionally.

Combine chicken broth, water, olive oil, vinegar, lemon juice, salt, pepper and sugar stirring well with a wire whisk. Pour over potato mixture. Add green onions, parsley, and capers; toss gently. Cover and chill at least 1 hour.

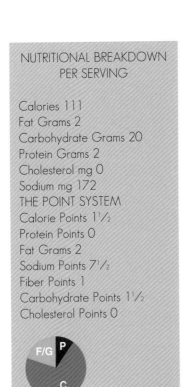

NUTRITIONAL BREAKDOWN
PER SERVING

Calories 111
Fat Grams 2
Carbohydrate Grams 20
Protein Grams 2
Cholesterol mg 0
Sodium mg 172
THE POINT SYSTEM
Calorie Points 1½
Protein Points 0
Fat Grams 2
Sodium Points 7½
Fiber Points 1
Carbohydrate Points 1½
Cholesterol Points 0

1 pound (460 g) fresh green beans, trimmed
and cut into 1" (2.5 cm) pieces
2 bulbs fresh fennel
½ pound (230 g) fresh mushrooms, cleaned,
trimmed and quartered
2 tablespoons lemon zest, grated
¼ cup (60 ml) balsamic vinegar
2 tablespoons water
2 tablespoons fresh lemon juice
2 tablespoons olive oil
1 teaspoon sugar
salt and freshly ground pepper

Green Beans and Fennel Salad

Serves: 8
Preparation Time: 45 minutes

Steam cleaned green beans in steamer 5 minutes (or use large frypan with grater steamer tray and 4 L dome cover). Run under cold water to stop cooking and drain. Place in salad bowl. Trim fennel leaves, reserve. Quarter bulb and remove core. Slice fennel bulb thinly and add to salad bowl. Quarter mushrooms and add to bowl. Add lemon zest. In small bowl combine vinegar, water, lemon juice, oil and sugar. Pour over salad and toss. Salt and pepper to taste. Finely mince reserved fennel leaves, sprinkle on top of salad. Cover and refrigerate 30 minutes.

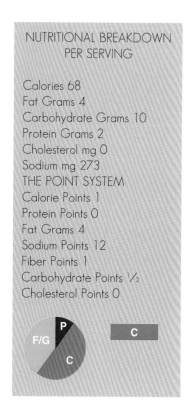

NUTRITIONAL BREAKDOWN
PER SERVING

Calories 68
Fat Grams 4
Carbohydrate Grams 10
Protein Grams 2
Cholesterol mg 0
Sodium mg 273
THE POINT SYSTEM
Calorie Points 1
Protein Points 0
Fat Grams 4
Sodium Points 12
Fiber Points 1
Carbohydrate Points ½
Cholesterol Points 0

Raita

Serves: 6
Preparation Time: 10 minutes

½	teaspoon salt (optional)
1	cup plain yogurt
1	clove garlic, minced
½	teaspoon ginger
2	teaspoons white vinegar
2	tablespoons mint leaves, chopped
¼	teaspoon black pepper, or to taste
¼	teaspoon garam masala*
2	cucumbers, sliced thin

* See recipe for Garam Masala in the Spice section, page 201.

Mix all ingredients except cucumbers. Just prior to serving add cucumbers and mix well.

The yogurt and cucumber mixture can take the fire out of hot spicy curry dishes. Serve as a small side salad.

NUTRITIONAL BREAKDOWN
PER SERVING

Calories 36
Fat Grams 0
Carbohydrate Grams 6
Protein Grams 3
Cholesterol mg 1
Sodium mg 143
THE POINT SYSTEM
Calorie Points ½
Protein Points 0
Fat Grams 0
Sodium Points 6
Fiber Points 0
Carbohydrate Points ½
Cholesterol Points 0

Company Tossed Salad

Serves: 8
Preparation Time: 15 minutes

1   large head green leaf
     or romaine lettuce
3   strips bacon, sliced ⅛" (0.5 cm)
2   cloves garlic, minced
¼   cup (60 ml) red wine vinegar dressing
     (San Francisco style is best)
4-5 mushrooms, sliced
     homemade croutons (recipe below)

Clean and dry greens in a salad spinner or on paper towels. Return to refrigerator covered with damp paper towel. Tear prior to mixing with other ingredients.

Brown bacon and garlic together in an 8" chef pan or small frypan over medium heat. Remove bacon and garlic from drippings with slotted spoon, drain on paper towels. Set chef pan with bacon drippings aside.

Just prior to serving, heat bacon drippings. Add prepared dressing to hot pan, deglazing pan. Pour over mixed greens and mushrooms. Toss well. Divide between individual bowls and top with reserved bacon bits and homemade croutons.

Homemade Croutons

Serves: 8
Preparation Time: 10 minutes

2   tablespoons low calorie
     margarine
1   teaspoon basil
1   teaspoon parsley flakes
½   teaspoon ground black pepper
4   slices toasted bread, cubed
2   tablespoons grated Parmesan
     cheese

Melt margarine in small frypan. Add basil, parsley, and pepper. Place bread in plastic bag and add Parmesan cheese. Pour margarine mixture over bread and shake to coat. May be stored in plastic bag in refrigerator up to one week.

NUTRITIONAL BREAKDOWN
PER SERVING
Calories 94
Fat Grams 5
Carbohydrate Grams 10
Protein Grams ½
Cholesterol mg 5
Sodium mg 180
THE POINT SYSTEM
Calorie Points 0
Protein Points 4
Fat Grams 5
Sodium Points 8
Fiber Points 0
Carbohydrate Points ½
Cholesterol Points 1½

Calories 43
Fat Grams 2
Carbohydrate Grams 5
Protein Grams 1
Cholesterol mg 1
Sodium mg 101
THE POINT SYSTEM
Calorie Points ½
Protein Points 0
Fat Grams 2
Sodium Points 4½
Fiber Points 0
Carbohydrate Points ½
Cholesterol Points 0

Italian Salad Dressing
Serves: 12 - 1 oz. servings
Preparation Time: 5 minutes

5	cloves garlic, minced
¾	cup (180 ml) olive oil
½	cup (120 ml) balsamic vinegar
⅓	cup (80 ml) red wine
2	teaspoons sugar
½	teaspoon salt
1	teaspoon pepper
1	tablespoon sweet basil
1	tablespoon parsley

Mix traditional salad ingredients with small can of sliced olives and ¼ cup shredded Parmesan. Mix all dressing ingredients together in a covered jar. Shake to blend. Pour desired amount of dressing over top and toss to coat.

NUTRITIONAL BREAKDOWN
PER SERVING
Calories 131
Fat Grams 14
Carbohydrate Grams 2
Protein Grams 0
Cholesterol mg 0
Sodium mg 94
THE POINT SYSTEM
Calorie Points 1½
Protein Points 0
Fat Grams 14
Sodium Points 4
Fiber Points 0
Carbohydrate Points 0
Cholesterol Points 0

Calories 198
Fat Grams 15
Carbohydrate Grams 17
Protein Grams 0
Cholesterol mg 0
Sodium mg 374
THE POINT SYSTEM
Calorie Points 2½
Protein Points 0
Fat Grams 15
Sodium Points 16
Fiber Points 0
Carbohydrate Points 1
Cholesterol Points 0

French Dressing
Yields: 15 - 3 tablespoon servings
Preparation Time: 10 minutes

1	10 3/4 ounce (305 g) can tomato soup
⅓	cup (80 ml) vinegar
¼	cup (60 ml) water
1	cup sugar
1	cup (240 ml) Mazola oil
½	tablespoon paprika
4	garlic cloves
½	tablespoon salt

Combine all of the ingredients in large jar. Mix or shake to blend. Can be used right after mixing. Shake before each use.

Southwest Vinegar

Yields: 10 cups ❖ Serves: 40
Preparation Time: 10 minutes (fermenting time 2 weeks)

1	large bunch fresh cilantro
12	fresh jalapeño peppers, unseeded, cut in half lengthwise
12	cloves garlic, cut in half lengthwise
1	lime, thinly sliced
12	dried tomato halves
1	teaspoon black peppercorns
5	17-ounce (2.5 L) bottles white wine vinegar
	Additional fresh cilantro sprigs and lime slices (optional)

Twist cilantro stems gently. Place cilantro and next 5 ingredients in a large glass container.

In 3-quart saucepan (3 L utensil), bring vinegar to a boil, and pour over cilantro mixture. Cover and let stand at room temperature 2 weeks.

Pour mixture through a large wire-mesh strainer into decorative bottles, discarding solids. Thread additional cilantro sprigs and lime slices on a wooden skewer, if desired, and place in bottle. Seal and store in a cool, dark place.

Tomato-Herb Vinegar

Yields: 11 cups ❖ Serves: 40
Preparation Time: 10 minutes (fermenting time 2 weeks)

10	large sprigs fresh rosemary
6	large sprigs fresh basil
4	large sprigs fresh oregano
12	cloves garlic, peeled and halved
10	dried tomato halves
1	teaspoon black peppercorns
3	32-ounce (1 L) bottles red wine vinegar
	Additional fresh rosemary (optional)

Twist stems of herbs gently, and press garlic with back of a spoon. Place herbs and garlic in a large glass container. Add tomatoes and peppercorns. Set aside.

In 4-quart saucepan (4 L utensil), bring vinegar to a boil and pour over herb mixture. Cover and let stand at room temperature 2 weeks.

Pour vinegar mixture through a large wire-mesh strainer into decorative bottles, discarding solids. Add additional rosemary, if desired. Seal bottles, and store in a cool, dry place.

NUTRITIONAL BREAKDOWN
PER SERVING
Calories 10
Fat Grams 0
Carbohydrate Grams 2
Protein Grams 1
Cholesterol mg 0
Sodium mg 110
THE POINT SYSTEM
Calorie Points 0
Protein Points 0
Fat Grams 0
Sodium Points 5
Fiber Points 0
Carbohydrate Points 0
Cholesterol Points 0

Calories 17
Fat Grams 0
Carbohydrate Grams 5
Protein Grams 0
Cholesterol mg 0
Sodium mg 3
THE POINT SYSTEM
Calorie Points 0
Protein Points 0
Fat Grams 0
Sodium Points 0
Fiber Points 0
Carbohydrate Points 0

Apricot Apple Chutney

Serves: 20
Preparation Time: 1 hour

1½	pounds (690 g) green apples
6	dried apricots
¾	cup (180 ml) water
1⅓	cups brown sugar
¼	cup raisins
1	onion, chopped
1	clove garlic, minced
⅔	cup (160 ml) cider vinegar
1	cinnamon stick
4	cloves
1	bay leaf
½	teaspoon garam masala*
1	teaspoon salt
½	teaspoon cayenne pepper

* See recipe for Garam Masala on page 201.

Peel, core and cut apples into small pieces. Rinse apricots with cold water and slice thin. Bring water to boil in 2-quart saucepan (2 L utensil). Add sugar and allow to dissolve. Add all remaining ingredients. Bring to boil, reduce to low and simmer uncovered 40 minutes. Remove cinnamon, cloves and bay leaf.

Excellent served with pork, lamb, chicken, or over toasted French bread.

NUTRITIONAL BREAKDOWN
PER SERVING

Calories 108
Fat Grams 0
Carbohydrate Grams 27
Protein Grams 0
Cholesterol mg 0
Sodium mg 115
THE POINT SYSTEM
Calorie Points 1½
Protein Points 0
Fat Grams 0
Sodium Points 5
Fiber Points 1
Carbohydrate Points 2
Cholesterol Points 0

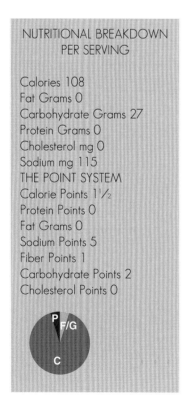

2	cloves garlic, minced
¼	cup onion, minced
1	tablespoon parsley, chopped
½	cup Velveeta Italian cheese
1	6 ounce (170 g) can crab meat, drained
12	large mushroom caps, stems removed
	paprika

Stuffed Mushrooms

Serves: 12
Preparation Time: 20 minutes

In small bowl, cut first five ingredients together with fork, or pulse in food processor adding crab last. Fill each mushroom cap with crab mixture. Place mushrooms in large frypan, cover, cook over medium heat until water seal is formed (approximately 5 minutes). Reduce to low heat for additional 10 minutes. Remove from pan to serving plates and sprinkle with paprika.

NUTRITIONAL BREAKDOWN
PER SERVING

Calories 43
Fat Grams 3
Carbohydrate Grams 2
Protein Grams 4
Cholesterol mg 15
Sodium mg 160
THE POINT SYSTEM
Calorie Points ½
Protein Points ½
Fat Grams 3
Sodium Points 7
Fiber Points 0
Carbohydrate Points 0
Cholesterol Points 1½

Hot Crab Dip

Serves: 15
Preparation Time: 15 minutes

⅓	cup Parmesan cheese
2	cups fat free mayonnaise
1	6 ounce (170 g) can Dungeness crab meat
1	13 ounce (370 g) jar artichoke hearts, drained and chopped
	tortilla chips
1	green onion, diced
¼	teaspoon cayenne pepper

Blend first 4 ingredients together in electric 3-quart saucepan (3 L utensil), heat through on low heat. Garnish top of dip with green onions and cayenne pepper. Serve with tortilla chips.*

*Tortilla chips not counted in nutritional breakdown. Refer to label on chip package.

NUTRITIONAL BREAKDOWN
PER SERVING

Calories 59
Fat Grams 1
Carbohydrate Grams 9
Protein Grams 4
Cholesterol mg 13
Sodium mg 527
THE POINT SYSTEM
Calorie Points 1
Protein Points 0
Fat Grams 1
Sodium Points 23
Fiber Points 0
Carbohydrate Points ½
Cholesterol Points 1

24   slices bacon, cut in half
      or Canadian bacon or prosciutto
1   can whole water chestnuts
1   cup (240 ml) reduced calorie ketchup
1   cup (240 ml) honey

Wrap one-half slice bacon around one whole chestnut,
secure with wooden toothpick. Repeat for remaining
chestnuts. Preheat 13" (33 cm) electric pan or chef pan
over medium heat. Add chestnuts, cover with vent open,
after 5 minutes turn. Drain any grease from pan, reduce to
low heat.

Combine ketchup and honey in medium bowl, pour over
wrapped chestnuts. Cover, continue cooking on low heat
for 10 minutes to glaze chestnuts.

Wrapped Chestnuts

Serves: 12
Preparation Time: 30 minutes

NUTRITIONAL BREAKDOWN
PER SERVING

Calories 227
Fat Grams 6
Carbohydrate Grams 38
Protein Grams 6
Cholesterol mg 11
Sodium mg 210
THE POINT SYSTEM
Calorie Points 3
Protein Points 1
Fat Grams 6
Sodium Points 9
Fiber Points 0
Carbohydrate Points 2½
Cholesterol Points 1

Sesame Chicken Wings

Serves: 8
Preparation Time: 25 minutes

12	chicken wings
1	tablespoon salted black beans
1	tablespoon water
2	cloves garlic, minced
2	slices fresh ginger, minced
3	tablespoons low sodium soy sauce
1½	tablespoons dry sherry or rice wine
¼	teaspoon black pepper
1	tablespoon sesame seeds
1	green onion, chopped

Cut off and discard wing tips using a sharp knife or kitchen shears. In small bowl, crush the beans and add the water, set aside. Heat wok or large frypan over medium-high heat; add chicken wings, garlic, and ginger. Lightly brown chicken. Add soy sauce and sherry, stir 30 seconds. Add the soaked black beans and pepper. Cover wok, reduce heat to medium and simmer 8-10 minutes.

Uncover, return heat to medium-high and continue to cook, occasionally stirring wings until liquid is almost evaporated and wings are glazed with sauce. Remove from heat, sprinkle on sesame seeds, stir to coat completely and serve. Garnish with green onion.

NUTRITIONAL BREAKDOWN
PER SERVING

Calories 173
Fat Grams 11
Carbohydrate Grams 2
Protein Grams 14
Cholesterol mg 44
Sodium mg 269
THE POINT SYSTEM
Calorie Points 2½
Protein Points 2
Fat Grams 11
Sodium Points 12
Fiber Points 0
Carbohydrate Points 0
Cholesterol Points 4

Hummus

2   cups chick peas, cooked
     or canned
¼   cup (60 ml) lemon juice
⅔   cup (160 ml) water
3   tablespoons vegetable oil
2   cloves garlic, minced
½   teaspoon salt
⅔   cup Tahini*

In blender puree chick peas with lemon juice, adding water
as needed to keep blender running. Add remaining ingredients, puree to creamy paste.

SERVING

Hummus may be served in many ways with a variety of garnishes. For a luncheon salad plate, arrange hummus on lettuce leaves. Sprinkle with paprika. Garnish plate with
sliced cucumbers, cherry tomatoes, carrot slices, and serve
with whole wheat bread or low-fat crackers.

For a sandwich spread, cut pieces of Middle Eastern flatbread** (pita) in half and fill the pockets with the hummus. Add garnishes such as shredded lettuce, chopped
tomatoes, chopped cucumber, etc., as you would garnish a
Mexican taco. Or spread on crackers or toast. For a raw
vegetable dip, serve with cut-up vegetables.

*See recipe for Tahini in the Spice section, page 201.

**See recipe for Nan Bread on page 162.

Serves: 8 ❖ Yields: 4 cups
Preparation Time: 10 minutes

NUTRITIONAL BREAKDOWN PER SERVING

Calories 211
Fat Grams 16
Carbohydrate Grams 14
Protein Grams 6
Cholesterol mg 2
Sodium mg 264
THE POINT SYSTEM
Calorie Points 3
Protein Points 1
Fat Grams 16
Sodium Points 11
Fiber Points 1½
Carbohydrate Points 1
Cholesterol Points 0

Beef • Lamb • Pork

Boeuf Bourguignon

2   pounds (1 kg) sirloin steak, in ¾" (2 cm) cubes
3   shallots, peeled and chopped
3   garlic cloves, chopped
     salt and pepper
4   tablespoons flour
3   cups (720 ml) dry red wine
1   bay leaf
2   cups (480 ml) beef stock, heated
1   teaspoon basil
1   teaspoon fresh parsley, chopped
2   tablespoons butter
24   pearl onions, peeled
1   pound (460 g) fresh mushrooms, cleaned and halved

Serves: 8
Preparation Time: 2½ hours

Preheat 6-quart (6 L) roaster over medium heat. Add meat and sear on all sides. Add shallots and garlic, cooking additional 5 minutes. Season with salt and pepper. Sprinkle flour over meat and mix well. Cook 4-5 minutes over medium heat.

Add wine and bay leaf and bring to a boil. Cook uncovered until reduced by two-thirds. Add beef stock and herbs; cover, reduce to low heat, simmer 2 hours. 30 minutes before end of cooking, heat butter in small frypan over medium heat. Add pearl onions and mushrooms, cook 5 minutes, then add to stew. Serve with toasted bread.

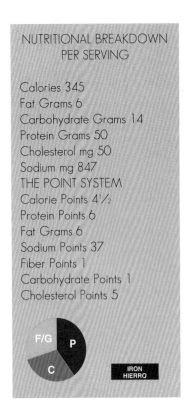

NUTRITIONAL BREAKDOWN
PER SERVING

Calories 345
Fat Grams 6
Carbohydrate Grams 14
Protein Grams 50
Cholesterol mg 50
Sodium mg 847
THE POINT SYSTEM
Calorie Points 4½
Protein Points 6
Fat Grams 6
Sodium Points 37
Fiber Points 1
Carbohydrate Points 1
Cholesterol Points .5

F/G   P

C

IRON
HIERRO

1	pound (460 g) lean round steak, ½" (1.5 cm) thick
2	cups fresh mushrooms, sliced
½	cup celery, chopped
3	green onions, chopped
1	clove garlic
2	8-ounce (230 g) cans no-salt-added tomato sauce
⅓	cup (80 ml) Chablis or other dry white wine
1	tablespoon lemon juice
1	bay leaf
½	teaspoon dried whole oregano
¼	teaspoon dried whole rosemary, crushed
⅛	teaspoon ground pepper
3	cups hot, cooked, unsalted medium egg noodles

Saucy Beef and Noodles

Serves: 6
Preparation Time: 1 hour

Trim excess fat from steak; cut meat into 1" (2.5 cm) pieces. Preheat 10" chef pan or large frypan over medium-high heat. Add steak and brown. Remove meat. Reduce heat to medium-low and add mushrooms, celery, green onions, and garlic. Sauté until vegetables are tender. Add meat, tomato sauce and next 6 ingredients; stir well. Cover; reduce heat to low, and simmer 45 minutes or until meat is tender. Remove and discard bay leaf. Serve over hot cooked noodles.

NUTRITIONAL BREAKDOWN
PER SERVING

Calories 309
Fat Grams 12
Carbohydrate Grams 29
Protein Grams 19
Cholesterol mg 73
Sodium mg 560
THE POINT SYSTEM
Calorie Points 4
Protein Points 2
Fat Grams 12
Sodium Points 3
Fiber Points 2
Charbohydrate Points 2
Cholesterol Points 7

F/G P
C

IRON
HIERRO

Beef with Broccoli

Serves: 6
Preparation Time: 1 hour 15 minutes

1	pound (460 g) lean round steak
2	tablespoons dry sherry, divided
2	teaspoons cornstarch
1	tablespoon cornstarch
2	teaspoons sugar, divided
2	teaspoons sesame oil
2	teaspoons reduced-sodium soy sauce, divided
1	pound (460 g) fresh broccoli
½	cup (120 ml) canned chicken broth, undiluted
1	tablespoon hoisin sauce
½	teaspoon ground white pepper
1	tablespoon safflower oil
1	tablespoon fresh ginger, minced
2	teaspoons fresh garlic, minced
1	medium sweet red pepper, in julienne strips
1	tablespoon sesame seeds, toasted
3	cups cooked rice

Partially freeze steak; slice diagonally across grain into ¼" (75 mm) strips. Combine 1 tablespoon dry sherry, 2 teaspoons cornstarch, 1 teaspoon sugar, 1 teaspoon sesame oil, 1 teaspoon soy sauce in large bowl; stir well. Add meat, tossing gently; cover and marinate in refrigerator 1 hour.

Trim off large leaves of broccoli and remove tough ends of lower stalks. Wash broccoli thoroughly. Cut off florets, and set aside. Cut stalks into ¼" (75 mm) slices; set aside.

Combine 1 tablespoon cornstarch and 1 tablespoon dry sherry in a small bowl; stir well. Add chicken broth, hoisin sauce, 1 teaspoon sugar, 1 teaspoon sesame oil, 1 teaspoon soy sauce, and white pepper; stir well and set aside.

Heat 13" (33 cm) electric pan or chef pan over medium-high heat. Add safflower oil; allow to heat 1 minute. Add ginger and garlic; stir-fry 30 seconds. Add beef and marinade; stir-fry 1 minute. Add broccoli and sweet red pepper; stir-fry 2 minutes. Add cornstarch mixture, stirring constantly. Cover, reduce heat to low, and cook 2 minutes or until mixture is lightly thickened. Sprinkle with sesame seeds. Serve immediately over cooked rice.

NUTRITIONAL BREAKDOWN PER SERVING

Calories 343
Fat Grams 9
Carbohydrate Grams 36
Protein Grams 31
Cholesterol mg 64
Sodium mg 348
THE POINT SYSTEM
Calorie Points 4½
Protein Points 4
Fat Grams 9
Sodium Points 15
Fiber Points 2½
Carbohydrate Points 2½
Cholesterol Points 6

8   wooden skewers
2   pounds (1 kg) rump roast
1   8 ounce (230 g) bottle reduced calorie
     Italian dressing
1   small package pearl onions
1   small package cherry tomatoes
1   small zucchini, 1" (2.5 cm) cubes
1   small package whole mushrooms
1   green pepper, 1" (2.5 cm) pieces

Griddle Kabobs

Serves: 8
Preparation Time: 45 minutes

Trim blunt end of skewers to width of griddle. Cut roast into 2" (5 cm) cubes and marinate in Italian dressing 30 minutes to 1 hour. While meat is marinating prepare rice or baked potatoes as side dish to serve with kabobs.

Skewer meat and vegetables. Preheat griddle over two burners on medium-high heat. Place kabobs carefully on griddle as they will immediately stick until seared. Turn after first side sears (approximately 4 minutes). Cook second side 4-5 minutes.

Baste with remaining marinade, if desired. Sprinkle with fresh ground pepper. Serve immediately with rice or baked potato.

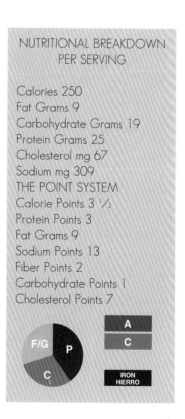

NUTRITIONAL BREAKDOWN
PER SERVING

Calories 250
Fat Grams 9
Carbohydrate Grams 19
Protein Grams 25
Cholesterol mg 67
Sodium mg 309
THE POINT SYSTEM
Calorie Points 3 1/2
Protein Points 3
Fat Grams 9
Sodium Points 13
Fiber Points 2
Carbohydrate Points 1
Cholesterol Points 7

Beef and Chinese Vegetables

Serves: 4
Preparation Time: 20 minutes

1	pound (460 g) lean beef round steak
⅔	cup green beans, sliced
⅔	cup carrots, sliced
⅔	cup turnips, sliced
⅔	cup cauliflower, sliced
⅔	cup Chinese cabbage, sliced
4	teaspoons cornstarch
½	teaspoon ground ginger
⅛	teaspoon garlic powder
1	tablespoon low sodium soy sauce
⅔	cup (160 ml) water

Trim fat from beef. Slice beef across the grain into ¼" (75 mm) strips. Clean and prepare all vegetables, rinse in 3-quart saucepan (3 L utensil), drain water leaving only what clings to vegetables. Cover and place over medium heat until seal forms. Reduce to low, simmer 5-10 minutes. Vegetables should be tender but still crisp.

While vegetables are cooking, preheat wok or large frypan over medium-high heat. Add beef and stir-fry about 2-3 minutes.

Mix cornstarch, ginger, garlic powder, soy sauce, and water. Stir cornstarch mixture into beef. Heat until sauce starts to boil. Serve meat sauce over vegetables.

NUTRITIONAL BREAKDOWN
PER SERVING

Calories 202
Fat Grams 5
Carbohydrate Grams 12
Protein Grams 27
Cholesterol mg 50
Sodium mg 243
THE POINT SYSTEM
Calorie Points 2½
Protein Points 3
Fat Grams 5
Sodium Points 10½
Fiber Points 1
Carbohydrate Points 1
Cholesterol Points 5

F/G
P
C

A
C

IRON
HIERRO

4	pork chops, trimmed of fat
1	medium onion, sliced and separated into rings
1	clove garlic, minced
1	16 ounce (460 g) can sauerkraut, drained
½	cup (120 ml) apple juice
1	teaspoon caraway seeds
¼	teaspoon ground thyme
¼	teaspoon pepper
1	small apple, cored and sliced

Sauerkraut and Pork Skillet

Serves: 4
Preparation Time: 45 minutes

Preheat large frypan over medium heat, add pork chops, brown both sides and remove from pan. Add onion rings and garlic. Cover, reduce heat to medium and cook for 10 minutes. Add sauerkraut, apple juice, caraway seeds, thyme and pepper. Stir to blend. Place chops on top; cover and simmer 20 minutes or until chops are tender. Add apple slices to pan; cover and simmer 5 minutes or until apple is just tender.

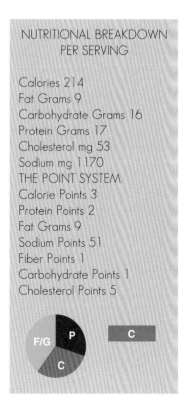

NUTRITIONAL BREAKDOWN
PER SERVING

Calories 214
Fat Grams 9
Carbohydrate Grams 16
Protein Grams 17
Cholesterol mg 53
Sodium mg 1170
THE POINT SYSTEM
Calorie Points 3
Protein Points 2
Fat Grams 9
Sodium Points 51
Fiber Points 1
Carbohydrate Points 1
Cholesterol Points 5

Swedish Meatballs

Serves: 4
Preparation Time: 30 minutes

1	pound (460 g) ground chuck*
1	egg
1	teaspoon garlic powder
½	teaspoon basil
¼	teaspoon oregano
¼	teaspoon parsley
2	tablespoons tomato paste
½	cup (120 ml) ketchup
¼	cup (60 ml) ginger ale
1	8 ounce (230 g) can evaporated milk
1	cup (240 ml) beef broth
	salt and pepper to taste

In large mixing bowl, combine ground chuck, egg, garlic powder, basil, oregano, and parsley. Mix thoroughly. Form mixture into 1" (2.5 cm) size balls. Preheat frypan over medium heat. Lightly brown meatballs. Meanwhile combine tomato paste, ketchup, ginger ale, evaporated milk and beef bouillon. Pour over meatballs, cover and cook over low heat 10 minutes. Serve over prepared noodles.

*Ground turkey or pork can be substituted for ground chuck.

NUTRITIONAL BREAKDOWN
PER SERVING

Calories 266
Fat Grams 9
Carbohydrate Grams 11
Protein Grams 36
Cholesterol mg 36
Sodium mg 828
THE POINT SYSTEM
Calorie Points 3½
Protein Points 4½
Fat Grams 9
Sodium Points 36
Fiber Points 0
Carbohydrate Points ½
Cholesterol Points 4

1	pound (460 g) ground beef
⅔	cup (160 ml) evaporated skim milk, divided
¼	cup (60 ml) ketchup
1	tablespoon dried parsley flakes
1	tablespoon prepared mustard
¼	teaspoon black pepper
1	10 ½ ounce (300 g) can cream of chicken soup
½	cup shredded Swiss cheese
¼	cup (60 ml) water
2-3	drops Tabasco

Meatballs á la Swiss

Serves: 4
Preparation Time: 30 minutes

Mix beef, ⅓ cup evaporated skim milk, ketchup, parsley flakes, mustard, and pepper. Shape into 16 meatballs, about 1½" (4 cm) in diameter. Preheat large frypan over medium heat. Lightly brown meatballs. Drain well. Mix soup, cheese, ⅓ cup evaporated skim milk, water, and Tabasco. Pour over meatballs. Cover, cooking over low heat 15 minutes or until bubbly. Serve over noodles or rice.

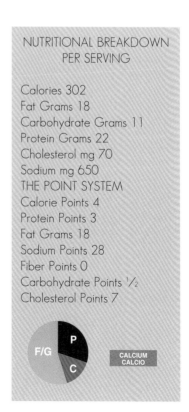

NUTRITIONAL BREAKDOWN
PER SERVING

Calories 302
Fat Grams 18
Carbohydrate Grams 11
Protein Grams 22
Cholesterol mg 70
Sodium mg 650
THE POINT SYSTEM
Calorie Points 4
Protein Points 3
Fat Grams 18
Sodium Points 28
Fiber Points 0
Carbohydrate Points ½
Cholesterol Points 7

P
F/G
C

CALCIUM
CALCIO

Italian Meatballs

Yields: 20 meatballs
Preparation Time: 1 hour

NUTRITIONAL BREAKDOWN PER SERVING

Calories 280
Fat Grams 13
Carbohydrate Grams 19
Protein Grams 21
Cholesterol mg 52
Sodium mg 473
THE POINT SYSTEM
Calorie Points 3½
Protein Points 3
Fat Grams 13
Sodium Points 20½
Fiber Points 1
Carbohydrate Points 1½
Cholesterol Points 5

SAUCE

1	tablespoon olive oil
½	cup onion, chopped
½	cup green pepper, chopped
2	cloves garlic, minced
2	16 ounce (460 g) cans whole tomatoes
1	cup (240 ml) tomato puree
1	teaspoon sugar
½	teaspoon oregano, fresh or dried
½	teaspoon basil, fresh or dried
½	pound (230 g) mushrooms, sliced

MEATBALLS

1	pound (460 g) ground chuck
½	pound (230 g) ground pork
½	cup grated Parmesan cheese
1	egg
½	cup bread crumbs
½	cup parsley, finely chopped
2-3	cloves garlic, minced
1	medium onion, finely chopped
	salt and pepper

For sauce, in a 6-quart (6 L) roaster sauté onion, green pepper and garlic in olive oil until softened. Add all remaining ingredients, mix well and simmer 1 hour, stirring occasionally.

Mix ingredients for meatballs in large bowl. Form into meatballs. Heat large frypan over medium heat. Add meatballs, turning as they brown. Drain on paper towels. Add to prepared sauce to finish cooking, approximately 15 minutes. Serve over prepared pasta of choice.

½	pound (230 g) lean ground beef
1	medium green pepper, finely chopped
1	medium onion, finely chopped
½	cup celery, finely chopped
¼	teaspoon Worcestershire sauce
¼	teaspoon pepper
1½	cups (360 ml) tomato juice
1	cup macaroni, uncooked
½	cup mushrooms, sliced

Ground Beef Skillet Casserole

Serves: 6
Preparation Time: 1 hour

Brown ground beef in large frypan over medium heat. Drain grease and add green pepper, onion and celery. Cook over medium heat 10 minutes. Add seasonings and remaining ingredients and combine thoroughly. Cover, reduce heat to low and simmer 40-45 minutes.

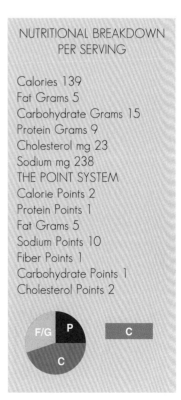

NUTRITIONAL BREAKDOWN
PER SERVING

Calories 139
Fat Grams 5
Carbohydrate Grams 15
Protein Grams 9
Cholesterol mg 23
Sodium mg 238
THE POINT SYSTEM
Calorie Points 2
Protein Points 1
Fat Grams 5
Sodium Points 10
Fiber Points 1
Carbohydrate Points 1
Cholesterol Points 2

Pork 'n Pineapple Chili

Serves: 12
Preparation Time: 3 hours

2	pounds (920 g) lean pork, cut into 1" (2.5 cm) pieces
3	cloves garlic, minced
2	medium onions, chopped
1	28 ounce (800 g) can chopped tomatoes
1	6 ounce (170 g) can tomato paste
1	4 ounce (120 g) can diced green chilis
1	green pepper, chopped
¼	cup chili powder
4	teaspoons cumin
1	tablespoon jalapeño chilis, diced
1	cup (240 ml) water
1	fresh pineapple cut into chunks
1	can white beans (optional)

Preheat 6-quart (6 L) roaster over medium heat. Brown pork cubes in two batches, drain on paper towel. Add garlic and onions to pan, sauté just until onions are tender. Add all remaining ingredients, stir, reduce to low, cover and simmer 2-3 hours. Optional: Add one can white beans 20 minutes before serving.

Serve with cornbread. Top each bowl with shredded cheddar cheese, green onions and 1 teaspoon sour cream.

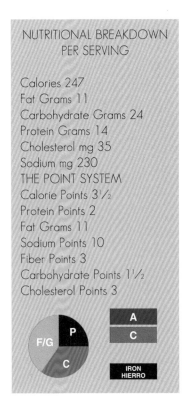

NUTRITIONAL BREAKDOWN
PER SERVING

Calories 247
Fat Grams 11
Carbohydrate Grams 24
Protein Grams 14
Cholesterol mg 35
Sodium mg 230
THE POINT SYSTEM
Calorie Points 3½
Protein Points 2
Fat Grams 11
Sodium Points 10
Fiber Points 3
Carbohydrate Points 1½
Cholesterol Points 3

2	pounds (1 kg) beef stew meat, trimmed of fat and cut into 1" (2.5 cm) cubes
2	cups (480 ml) dry red wine
2	cloves garlic, minced
½	teaspoon dried rosemary, crushed
½	teaspoon dried thyme, crushed
2	teaspoons orange peel, finely shredded
¼	teaspoon pepper
½	cup (120 ml) water
6	carrots, 1" (2.5 cm) slices
6	small onions, halved
6	new potatoes, quartered
1	cup fresh mushrooms, sliced
¼	head red cabbage, coarsely shredded
1	green pepper, chopped
1	15 ounce (425 g) can stewed tomatoes
2	tablespoons cornstarch
2	tablespoons cold water

Blarney Stone Stew

Serves: 12
Preparation Time: 1½-2 hours

Preheat 4-quart saucepan (4 L utensil) over medium heat, add stew meat and brown lightly. Add wine, garlic, rosemary, thyme, orange peel, pepper, and ½ cup (120 ml) water. Bring to a boil. Cover, reduce to low and simmer 1 hour. Add carrots, onions, potatoes, mushrooms, red cabbage, green pepper, and stewed tomatoes; cover and continue to cook 30 to 40 minutes more or until meat and vegetables are tender. Add combined cornstarch and 2 tablespoons cold water to thicken stew. Garnish with snipped parsley, if desired. Serve with Irish Soda Bread, page 175.

NUTRITIONAL BREAKDOWN
PER SERVING

Calories 252
Fat Grams 4
Carbohydrate Grams 26
Protein Grams 22
Cholesterol mg 47
Sodium mg 176
THE POINT SYSTEM
Calorie Points 3½
Protein Points 3
Fat Grams 4
Sodium Points 8
Fiber Points 2
Carbohydrate Points 1½
Cholesterol Points 5

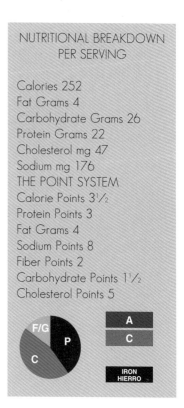

Marinated Flank Steak

2   pounds (1 kg) flank steak
2   cloves garlic, minced
¼   cup onion, minced
¼   cup (60 ml) olive oil
1   lemon, juice of
½   cup (120 ml) red wine
3   tablespoons balsamic vinegar
1   tablespoon dried oregano
3   tablespoons dried parsley

Lightly score flank steak on both sides against the grain of the meat. Mix all other ingredients in bowl to marinate meat. Place steak in bowl, turning to coat, cover and refrigerate until ready to cook. The longer the steak marinates the better; however, 30 minutes flavors the meat well.

Preheat large frypan over medium-high heat until water drops "dance" when sprinkled in pan. Remove flank steak from marinade and place in hot pan, allowing some garlic and onion to remain on steak. Sear meat until it releases from first side, approximately 4 minutes. Turn, reduce heat, and sear second side, cover for 4 minutes for rare, or longer to desired doneness.

Deglaze pan with marinade mixture. Pour over flank steak. Slice diagonally across the grain in ¼" (1 cm) strips.

Serve with baked potatoes or rice.

Serves: 8
Preparation Time: 40 minutes

NUTRITIONAL BREAKDOWN PER SERVING

Calories 440
Fat Grams 25
Carbohydrate Grams 5
Protein Grams 44
Cholesterol mg 75
Sodium mg 110
THE POINT SYSTEM
Calorie Points 6
Protein Points 5½
Fat Grams 25
Sodium Points 5
Fiber Points 0
Carbohydrate Points 0
Cholesterol Points 7½

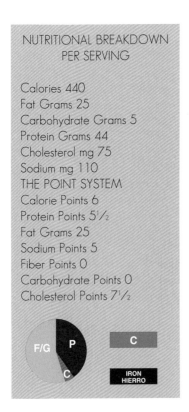

Meatloaf

1½ pounds (700 g) ground veal, lamb,
beef, pork, or chicken
or a mixture of these
½ onion, finely chopped
½ green pepper, chopped
1 stalk celery, chopped
1 cup bread crumbs or oatmeal
½ teaspoon oregano
1 teaspoon basil
1 egg
salt and pepper to taste

Place all ingredients in a bowl, mix together. Press loaf
into cool frypan. Top with ketchup or tomato sauce, if
desired. Cover and cook over medium heat 15 minutes,
reduce to low, cook an additional 40 minutes or until done.

If you are limiting the red meat in your diet; meatloaf is a
wonderful recipe to substitute TVP (textured vegetable
protein) for ground beef. Check with your local natural
food store for availability.

Serves: 8
Preparation Time: 1 hour

NUTRITIONAL BREAKDOWN
PER SERVING

Calories 229
Fat Grams 12
Carbohydrate Grams 12
Protein Grams 17
Cholesterol mg 53
Sodium mg 441
THE POINT SYSTEM
Calorie Points 3
Protein Points 2
Fat Grams 12
Sodium Points 19
Fiber Points 0
Carbohydrate Points 1
Cholesterol Points 5

Basic Lasagna

pictured with Meat Sauce at right

Serves: 16
Preparation Time: 1 hour

4	cups (1 L) meat sauce (see page 85)	
1	8 ounce (230 g) box lasagna noodles, uncooked	
1	16 ounce (460 g) carton low-fat ricotta cheese	
2	cups skim mozzarella cheese, grated	
½	cup Parmesan cheese, grated	

Pour one cup of meat sauce into bottom of 13" (33 cm) electric pan or chef pan. Place one layer of uncooked lasagna noodles on top. Continue layering in the following order: 1 cup meat sauce, the ricotta cheese, 1 cup mozzarella cheese, 1 cup meat sauce, another layer of noodles, 1 cup sauce, 1 cup mozzarella cheese and finally Parmesan cheese on top. Cover.

FOR ELECTRIC PAN:
Turn electric pan to 225°F (110°C) and cook for 35-45 minutes covered, vent closed. Unplug, uncover, let stand for 10 minutes before serving.

FOR 13" (33 CM) CHEF PAN
Turn heat to medium for 5 minutes. Reduce to low and cook for 35 minutes. Remove from heat, uncover and let stand 10 minutes before serving.

Serve with Garlic Bread, recipe on page 175.

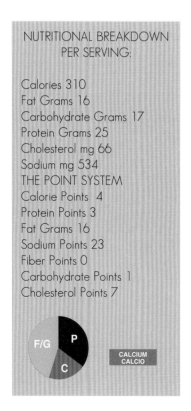

NUTRITIONAL BREAKDOWN
PER SERVING:

Calories 310
Fat Grams 16
Carbohydrate Grams 17
Protein Grams 25
Cholesterol mg 66
Sodium mg 534
THE POINT SYSTEM
Calorie Points 4
Protein Points 3
Fat Grams 16
Sodium Points 23
Fiber Points 0
Carbohydrate Points 1
Cholesterol Points 7

Meat Sauce

Serves: 8
Preparation Time: 35 minutes

2 pounds (1 kg) lean ground beef
1 onion, chopped
2 cloves garlic, minced
1 28 ounce (800 g) can plum tomatoes, diced
1 12 ounce (350 g) can tomato sauce
1 tablespoon oregano flakes
2 tablespoons dried sweet basil
1 tablespoon dried parsley
2 tablespoons sugar
   salt and pepper to taste

Brown ground beef in 6-quart (6 L) roaster over medium heat. Drain fat drippings. Add onion and garlic to meat, cover and cook over low heat 10 minutes. Add all other ingredients, continue cooking over low heat 15 minutes. Salt and pepper to taste. Use in basic lasagna recipe or over your favorite pasta. Sprinkle with freshly grated Parmesan or Romano cheese.

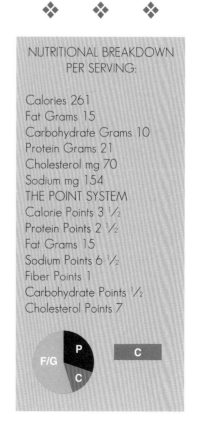

NUTRITIONAL BREAKDOWN
PER SERVING:

Calories 261
Fat Grams 15
Carbohydrate Grams 10
Protein Grams 21
Cholesterol mg 70
Sodium mg 154
THE POINT SYSTEM
Calorie Points 3 ½
Protein Points 2 ½
Fat Grams 15
Sodium Points 6 ½
Fiber Points 1
Carbohydrate Points ½
Cholesterol Points 7

BBQ Baby Back Ribs

Serves: 10
Preparation Time: 3 hours

6   pounds (3 kg) baby back pork loin ribs

BOILING MIXTURE:
5   quarts (5 L) water
1   onion, cut into 1" (2.5 cm) chunks
4   celery ribs, cut into 1" (2.5 cm) chunks
2   cups (480 ml) Burgundy cooking wine

BARBECUE SAUCE:
½   cup green pepper, chopped
1   onion, chopped
¼   cup (60 ml) water
1½   cups brown sugar
1   cup (240 ml) molasses
¼   cup (60 ml) mustard
2   tablespoons Tobasco sauce
¼   teaspoon liquid smoke
2   teaspoons Worcestershire sauce
2   cups (480 ml) prepared barbecue sauce
1¾   cups (420 ml) ketchup

Put whole racks of ribs into pasta pan or 6-quart (6 L) utensil and cover with water. Add the onion, celery and Burgundy wine. Cover, bring to a boil and simmer for 1½-2 hours or until meat is tender and pulls easily away from the bones.

For the sauce, run green pepper and onion through blender with the water until smooth. Pour into 3-quart saucepan (3 L utensil). Add all other ingredients; stir and cook over low heat uncovered for 45 minutes.

When ribs are tender, drain and remove from pan to dry. When BBQ sauce has simmered, remove from heat to cool. Both items may be made in advance and refrigerated until needed.

Dip whole rib rack into BBQ sauce or paint on with brush. Place in large chef pan. Preheat in oven at 350°F (180°C) 15 minutes or until ribs are glazed and appear candied.

Place cooked rib rack on cutting board. Cut between the bones. Serve entire rack on a plate with a side of BBQ sauce for dipping.

NUTRITIONAL BREAKDOWN
PER SERVING

Calories 551
Fat Grams 27
Carbohydrate Grams 46
Protein Grams 26
Cholesterol mg 62
Sodium mg 608
THE POINT SYSTEM
Calorie Points 7½
Protein Points 3
Fat Grams 27
Sodium Points 26½
Fiber Points 0
Carbohydrate Points 3
Cholesterol Points 6

C P
F/G

C
CALCIUM
CALCIO
IRON
HIERRO

Beef Fajitas

Yields: 12 fajitas ❖ Serves: 6
Preparation Time: 1 hour 15 minutes

MARINADE

4   garlic cloves, minced and mashed to a paste
       with 1 teaspoon salt
¼   cup (60 ml) fresh lime juice
1½   teaspoons ground cumin
2   tablespoons olive oil

2   pounds (1 kg) flank steak
2   tablespoons vegetable oil
3   assorted colored bell peppers, sliced thin
1   large red onion, sliced thin
2   garlic cloves, minced
12   7-inch flour tortillas, warmed
       guacamole and tomato salsa as accompaniments

Prepare the marinade by whisking together in a large bowl the garlic paste, lime juice, cumin, and oil. Add the steak to marinade, turning it to coat it well, and let it marinate, covered and chilled, for at least 1 hour or overnight.

To grill steak, preheat 13" (33 cm) chef pan over medium-high heat. Add steak whole to pan, sear first side 4 minutes, turn and sear second side. Transfer the steak to a cutting board and let it stand for 10 minutes.

In large frypan heat the oil over moderately high heat until it is hot but not smoking, add the bell peppers, onion and garlic. Sauté the mixture, stirring, for 5 minutes or until the bell peppers are softened. Slice the steak thin across the grain on the diagonal and arrange the slices on a platter with bell pepper mixture. Drizzle any steak juices over steak and bell pepper mixture. Serve with tortillas, guacamole, and salsa.

To assemble a fajita: Spread some of the guacamole on a tortilla, top it with a few slices of steak, some of the bell pepper mixture and some salsa and roll up tortilla to enclose filling.

Flour Tortillas

Yields: 12-7 (18 cm) inch tortillas
Preparation Time: 45-50 minutes

TORTILLAS

2	cups all-purpose flour
¼	cup cold vegetable shortening, cut into pieces
1	teaspoon salt

In a bowl blend the flour and the shortening until the mixture resembles fine meal. In a small bowl stir together salt and ⅔ cup warm water, add salted water to flour mixture, and toss mixture until liquid is incorporated. Form dough into a ball and knead it on a lightly floured surface for 2-3 minutes, or until it is smooth. Divide the dough into 12 equal pieces, form each piece into a ball, and let dough stand, covered with plastic wrap, for at least 30 minutes and up to 1 hour.

Heat a 10" chef pan or large frypan over moderately high heat until it is hot. On a lightly floured surface roll one ball of dough at a time into a 7" (18 cm) round. Place the tortilla in the pan, turning it once, for 1 ½ minutes, or until it is puffy and golden on both sides. Wrap tortilla in a kitchen towel and prepare more tortillas with remaining dough in same manner, stacking and enclosing them in towel as they are done. The tortillas may be made 1 day in advance and kept chilled in a plastic bag.

TO WARM TORTILLAS:

If tortillas are very dry to begin with, pat each tortilla between dampened hands before stacking them. Stack in frypan, cover, place on warm burner 10 minutes.

NUTRITIONAL BREAKDOWN
PER SERVING:

Calories 114
Fat Grams 4
Carbohydrate Grams 16
Protein Grams 2
Cholesterol mg 0
Sodium mg 178
THE POINT SYSTEM
Calorie Points 1 ½
Protein Points 0
Fat Grams 4
Sodium Points 8
Fiber Points 0
Carbohydrate Points 1

Guacamole

Serves: 8
Preparation Time: 15 minutes

2	ripe avocados
1	small onion, minced
1	garlic clove, minced and mashed to a paste with ½ teaspoon salt
4	teaspoons fresh lime juice, or to taste
½	teaspoon ground cumin
1	plum tomato, diced
3	tablespoons chopped fresh coriander, if desired

Halve and pit the avocados and scoop the flesh into a bowl. Mash the avocados coarse with a fork and stir in the onion, garlic paste, lime juice, cumin, tomato, and the coriander. The guacamole may be made 2 hours in advance and kept chilled, its surface covered with plastic wrap.

Tomato Salsa

Serves: 8
Preparation Time: 15 minutes

1	pound (460 g) tomatoes, peeled if desired, seeded, and chopped
1	small onion, minced
1	tablespoon fresh lime juice
2	tablespoons chopped fresh coriander, if desired
1	jalapeño chili, minced (optional)

In bowl toss together the tomatoes, onion, lime juice, coriander, jalapeño chili (optional), and salt to taste and let the salsa stand for 30 minutes. The salsa may be made 4 hours in advance and kept covered and chilled. Let the salsa come to room temperature before serving.

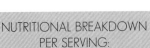

NUTRITIONAL BREAKDOWN
PER SERVING:

Calories 62
Fat Grams 5
Carbohydrate Grams 5
Protein Grams 1
Cholesterol mg 0
Sodium mg 8
THE POINT SYSTEM
Calorie Points 1
Protein Points 0
Fat Grams 5
Sodium Points 0
Fiber Points ½
Carbohydrate Points ½

Calories 22
Fat Grams 0
Carbohydrate Grams 5
Protein Grams 1
Cholesterol mg 0
Sodium mg 16
THE POINT SYSTEM
Calorie Points ½
Protein Points 0
Fat Grams 0
Sodium Points 1
Fiber Points ½
Carbohydrate Points ½

FILLING

6	large cabbage leaves
½	pound (230 g) ground turkey
½	pound (230 g) lean ground pork
1	cup cooked rice
½	cup onion, chopped
½	teaspoon basil
½	teaspoon parsley
¼	teaspoon oregano
⅛	teaspoon garlic powder
⅛	teaspoon salt
⅛	teaspoon pepper

SAUCE

1	8-ounce (230 g) can tomato sauce
½	teaspoon basil
½	teaspoon parsley
¼	teaspoon oregano

Steam whole head of cabbage in large steamer covered over boiling water just until leaves wilt, approximately 7-10 minutes. Set aside to cool.

Combine turkey, pork, rice, onion, and spices in large bowl, mix well. Place ½ cup mixture in center of each cabbage leaf, fold ends of leaf over and roll up. Place in large frypan seam side down. Mix sauce ingredients together and pour evenly over cabbage rolls. Cover pan, place over medium-low heat 45 minutes to 1 hour or until done.

Stuffed Cabbage Rolls

Serves: 6
Preparation Time: 1 hour, 15 minutes

NUTRITIONAL BREAKDOWN
PER SERVING:

Calories 188
Fat Grams 8
Carbohydrate Grams 12
Protein Grams 17
Cholesterol mg 55
Sodium mg 124
THE POINT SYSTEM
Calorie Points 2½
Protein Points 2
Fat Grams 8
Sodium Points 5
Fiber Points 0
Carbohydrate Points 1
Cholesterol Points 5

Stuffed Peppers

Serves: 4
Preparation Time: 40 minutes

4	medium green bell peppers
½	cup onion, chopped
1	celery rib, chopped
1	clove garlic, minced
1	tablespoon olive oil
½	pound (230 g) lean ground round
1	cup rice, cooked
1	8 ounce (230 g) can tomato sauce
1	2½ ounce (75 g) jar sliced mushrooms
½	teaspoon oregano
1	teaspoon sweet basil

Remove tops and seed green peppers. In large frypan over medium heat, sauté onion, celery and garlic in olive oil until tender. Add ground round and brown. Add all other ingredients and stir until well blended. Spoon mixture into bell peppers. Stand filled peppers upright in 3-quart saucepan (3 L utensil). Add 3 tablespoons water, cover and cook on low heat until peppers are heated through and tender, approximately 30 minutes.

NUTRITIONAL BREAKDOWN
PER SERVING:

Calories 258
Fat Grams 11
Carbohydrate Grams 26
Protein Grams 14
Cholesterol mg 35
Sodium mg 471
THE POINT SYSTEM:
Calorie Points 3½
Protein Points 2
Fat Grams 11
Sodium Points 20½
Fiber Points 2
Carbohydrate Points 2
Cholesterol Points 3

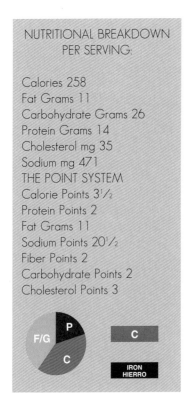

1	cup all-purpose flour
4	tablespoons cornstarch
1½	teaspoons baking powder
1	pinch salt
1	tablespoon oil
	water
8	ounces (230 g) pork tenderloin, cut into ½" (1.5 cm) cubes
1	onion, sliced
1	green pepper, seeded, cored and sliced
1	small can pineapple chunks, juice reserved oil for frying

Sweet and Sour Pork

Serves: 6
Preparation Time: 30 minutes

❖   ❖   ❖

SWEET AND SOUR SAUCE

2	tablespoons cornstarch
½	cup light brown sugar
1	pinch salt
½	cup (120 ml) cider vinegar or rice vinegar
1	clove garlic, crushed
1	teaspoon fresh ginger, grated
6	tablespoons tomato ketchup
6	tablespoons reserved pineapple juice

To prepare the batter, sift the flour, cornstarch, baking powder and salt into a bowl. Make a well in the center and add the oil and enough water to make a thick, smooth batter. Using a wooden spoon, stir the ingredients in the well, gradually incorporating flour from the outside, and beat until smooth.

Heat enough oil in wok or large frypan to deep-fry the pork. Dip the pork cubes one at a time into the batter and drop into the hot oil. Fry 4-5 pieces of pork at a time and remove them with a slotted spoon to paper towels. Continue until all the pork is fried.

Pour off oil from the wok and add the sliced onion, pepper and pineapple. Cook over medium-high heat for 1-2 minutes. Remove and set aside.

Mix all the sauce ingredients together and pour into the wok. Bring slowly to a boil, stirring continuously until thickened. Allow to simmer for about 1-2 minutes or until completely clear.

Add the vegetables, pineapple, and pork cubes to the sauce and stir to coat completely. Reheat for 1-2 minutes and serve immediately.

NUTRITIONAL BREAKDOWN
PER SERVING:

Calories 324
Fat Grams 6
Carbohydrate Grams 57
Protein Grams 12
Cholesterol mg 22
Sodium mg 325
THE POINT SYSTEM
Calorie Points 4½
Protein Points 1½
Fat Grams 6
Sodium Points 14
Fiber Points 1
Carbohydrate Points 4
Cholesterol Points 2

Pork & Shrimp Pot Stickers

Serves: 12
Yields: 48 Pot Stickers
Preparation Time: 1 hour, 15 minutes

Pot Stickers take a little time to prepare but the final taste treat is well worth it. Chop finely the ingredients listed below. The ingredients for filling make 48 pot stickers; however, the instructions are for cooking them 12 at a time.

3	cups flour
¼	teaspoon salt
1	cup (240 ml) warm water
½	pound (230 g) shrimp, peeled and shelled
½	pound (230 g) ground pork
1	cup cabbage, chopped
3	green onions, minced
¼	cup mushrooms, minced
2	tablespoons soy sauce
1	clove of garlic, minced
1⅓	cups (320 ml) low sodium chicken broth, divided

Mix flour, salt and warm water in bowl. On unfloured board, knead dough until very smooth and satiny. Cover and let rest ½ hour.

Prepare the filling. Combine shrimp, pork, cabbage, onions, mushrooms, soy sauce and garlic. Mix well.

Divide dough into two portions, keeping half covered to keep it from drying out. Roll out dough to ⅛" (50 mm) thickness. Cut out 3" (7.5 cm) circles, place filling in center of circle. Fold in half over filling pinching the edges closed, making a few tucks along the edge. Cover finished pot stickers and complete other half.

Spray large frypan with cooking spray or lightly oil. Place over medium heat cooking 12 pot stickers at a time. Cook until bottoms are golden brown.

Pour ⅓ cup of chicken broth over the pot stickers, reduce to low, and cover to steam 15 minutes. Remove cover, allow any remaining moisture to evaporate. Repeat process for additional pot stickers or they may be frozen before frying for later use. Serve with Soy Dipping Sauce on pg 153.

1½	pounds (700 g) pork tenderloin, trimmed of fat and cut into 1½" (4 cm) cubes
2	teaspoons olive oil
2	teaspoons whole cumin seed
1	large onion, coarsely chopped
3	cloves garlic, minced
1	14-ounce (400 g) can whole tomatoes, crushed (with juice)
1	cup (240 ml) defatted reduced-sodium chicken stock
½	cup (120 ml) dry white wine
½	teaspoon dried oregano
¼	teaspoon red pepper flakes
1	pound (460 g) fresh pumpkin or butternut squash, peeled and cut into 1" (2.5 cm) chunks (3 cups)
1	tablespoon cornstarch
1	tablespoon water
3	tablespoons fresh parsley or cilantro, chopped salt and freshly ground black pepper to taste
2	tablespoons pumpkin seeds (pepitas), lightly toasted (optional)

Pork and Pumpkin Stew

Serves: 6
Preparation Time: 1 hour

Preheat 6-quart (6 L) roaster over medium-high heat. Add one-half of pork cubes to the pan, browning on all sides, transfer to a plate and brown remaining half, transferring to plate. Reduce heat to low, add oil and cumin, sauté 30 seconds, add onion and garlic, sauté 2 minutes. Add tomatoes, chicken stock, wine, oregano, red pepper flakes and reserved pork. Cover, and continue to cook over low heat 30 minutes. Add pumpkin or squash, cover and continue to cook another 15 minutes. Dissolve cornstarch in water, add to stew to thicken, stirring gently. Add cilantro or parsley, salt and pepper. Serve with rice, garnished with toasted pumpkin seeds.

NUTRITIONAL BREAKDOWN
PER SERVING:

Calories 314
Fat Grams 13
Carbohydrate Grams 18
Protein Grams 30
Cholesterol mg 65
Sodium mg 222
THE POINT SYSTEM
Calorie Points 4
Protein Points 4
Fat Grams 13
Sodium Points 10
Fiber Points 1
Carbohydrate Points 1
Cholesterol Points 6

Poultry

Lemon-Sesame Chicken

Serves: 4
Preparation Time: 20 minutes

4 skinless chicken breasts
1 fresh lemon
1 tablespoon sesame seeds
1 teaspoon oregano

Preheat large frypan over medium-high heat.

Place skinless chicken breast-side down in the pan, reduce heat to medium. Cover the pan and leave vent open or leave cover slightly ajar. Cook 10 minutes on one side until browned, turn the chicken over, cover and cook for another 5-7 minutes or until done.

Place on serving dish. Squeeze the fresh lemon over the chicken and sprinkle it with the sesame seeds and oregano. Serve immediately.

NUTRITIONAL BREAKDOWN
PER SERVING

Calories 304
Fat Grams 7
Carbohydrate Grams 4
Protein Grams 54
Cholesterol mg 146
Sodium mg 127
THE POINT SYSTEM
Calorie Points 4
Protein Points 7
Fat Grams 7
Sodium Points 6
Fiber Points 0
Carbohydrate Points 1/2
Cholesterol Points 15

4	pounds (2 kg) bone-in chicken pieces, skinned
40	large cloves garlic, unpeeled (about 4 heads)
1¾	cups (420 ml) dry white wine
¼	teaspoon (4 sprigs) thyme, fresh
¼	teaspoon (1 sprig) rosemary, fresh
2	tablespoons Cognac
	fresh parsley, chopped
12	slices coarse bread, toasted

Chicken and Roasted Garlic

Heat large 13" (33 cm) chef pan over medium heat until a water drops "dance" when sprinkled in the pan. Add chicken and brown first side, turning after chicken releases itself from the pan (about 5-8 minutes), then turn to brown second side. Remove chicken pieces from the pan. Add garlic, stirring, for 3-5 minutes, until beginning to brown. Spread cloves in a single layer and return the chicken pieces to the pan. Add wine, thyme and rosemary, and cover. Cook over low heat 30 minutes.

Pour cognac over the chicken and sprinkle with fresh parsley. Remove chicken pieces to platter or serve directly from chef pan. Serve the toasted bread with garlic cloves.

Note: When the garlic is squeezed out of its natural wrapper it spreads like butter on the bread.

Serves: 6
Preparation Time: 50 minutes

❖   ❖   ❖

NUTRITIONAL BREAKDOWN
PER SERVING:

Calories 250
Fat Grams 6
Carbohydrate Grams 18
Protein Grams 22
Cholesterol mg 58
Sodium mg 251
THE POINT SYSTEM
Calorie Points 3
Protein Points 3
Fat Grams 6
Sodium Points 11
Fiber Points 2
Carbohydrate Points 1
Cholesterol Points 6

Lemon Baked Chicken

Serves: 4
Preparation Time: 50 minutes

4	chicken breast halves, skinless
3	tablespoons lemon juice
2	tablespoons water
¼	teaspoon onion powder
¼	teaspoon marjoram leaves
¼	teaspoon salt
⅛	teaspoon paprika
	parsley to taste

Preheat 10" chef pan or large frypan over medium heat until water drops "dance" when sprinkled in pan. Brown chicken on both sides. Mix all other ingredients and pour over browned chicken. Cover, reduce heat to low, and simmer 30 minutes.

Serve with snow peas and toasted sesame seeds.

NUTRITIONAL BREAKDOWN
PER SERVING:

Calories 298
Fat Grams 6
Carbohydrate Grams 4
Protein Grams 54
Cholesterol mg 146
Sodium mg 261
THE POINT SYSTEM
Calorie Points 4
Protein Points 7
Fat Grams 6
Sodium Points 11
Fiber Points 0
Carbohydrate Points 0
Cholesterol Points 15

3	whole chicken breasts halved, skinned
1	cup celery, finely chopped
1	whole onion, finely chopped
2	cloves garlic, minced
½	green pepper, chopped
½	sweet red pepper, chopped
½	cup fresh mushrooms, sliced
1	16 ounce (460 g) can whole tomatoes, halved
1	15 ounce (425 g) can tomato sauce
1	cup uncooked long-grain rice
2	cups (480 ml) low sodium chicken broth
1	cup water

Chicken Cacciatore

Serves: 6
Preparation Time: 40 minutes

Preheat large frypan over medium heat until water drops "dance" when sprinkled in the pan. Add chicken, cover and brown first side turning after chicken releases itself from the pan (5-8 minutes), then turn to brown second side. Remove from pan. Add celery, onion, garlic, green and red pepper, mushrooms, tomatoes, and tomato sauce. Stir to mix. Place browned chicken on top; simmer covered 15-20 minutes.

In 2-quart saucepan (2 L utensil) cook rice according to package directions, using chicken broth and water mixture.

Serve chicken and sauce over rice. Season to taste.

NUTRITIONAL BREAKDOWN
PER SERVING:

Calories 346
Fat Grams 5
Carbohydrate Grams 45
Protein Grams 35
Cholesterol mg 73
Sodium mg 284
THE POINT SYSTEM
Calorie Points 4 ½
Protein Points 4
Fat Grams 5
Sodium Points 12
Fiber Points 3
Carbohydrate Points 3
Cholesterol Points 7

Evening Parmesan Chicken

Serves: 6
Preparation Time: 45 minutes

6	chicken breast halves, skinned
¾	cup fine dry bread crumbs
⅓	cup Parmesan cheese, grated
3	tablespoons fresh parsley, chopped
¼	teaspoon pepper
½	cup (120 ml) Italian dressing (reduced calorie may be used)

Preheat large frypan over medium heat until water drops "dance" when sprinkled in the pan. Add chicken, cover and brown first side, turning after chicken releases itself from the pan (5-8 minutes), then turn to brown second side. Remove chicken to platter.

Combine dry ingredients, set aside. Dip chicken in salad dressing then roll in bread crumb mixture. Return breaded chicken to pan, cover and cook over low heat 30 minutes.

NUTRITIONAL BREAKDOWN

PER SERVING:
Calories 384
Fat Grams 11
Carbohydrate Grams 11
Protein Grams 57
Cholesterol mg 152
Sodium mg 503
THE POINT SYSTEM
Calorie Points 5
Protein Points 7
Fat Grams 11
Sodium Points 22
Fiber Points 0
Carbohydrate Points 1
Cholesterol Points 15

6	chicken thighs, skinned
1	cup fresh mushrooms, sliced
4	green onions, chopped
1	clove garlic, minced
½	cup (120 ml) Chablis or other dry white wine
¼	teaspoon whole thyme, dried
	or 1 teaspoon fresh thyme, chopped
2	medium tomatoes cut into wedges
1	tablespoon fresh parsley, minced

Chicken Thighs Marengo

Serves: 6
Preparation Time: 45 minutes

Trim excess fat from chicken. Rinse chicken with cold water and pat dry. Preheat large frypan over medium heat until water drops "dance" when sprinkled in the pan. Add chicken, cover and brown first side, turning after chicken releases itself from the pan (5-8 minutes), then turn to brown second side. Remove chicken to platter. Add mushrooms to pan and cook 2 minutes, stirring frequently. Remove mushrooms and set aside.

Add onions and garlic to pan and sauté 1 minute. Stir in wine and thyme. Add reserved chicken. Bring mixture to a boil. Cover; reduce heat to low and simmer 25 minutes. Add reserved mushrooms and tomato wedges; simmer 2 minutes or until thoroughly heated. Sprinkle with parsley and serve immediately.

NUTRITIONAL BREAKDOWN
PER SERVING:

Calories 136
Fat Grams 6
Carbohydrate Grams 3
Protein Grams 14
Cholesterol mg 49
Sodium mg 52
THE POINT SYSTEM
Calorie Points 2
Protein Points 2
Fat Grams 6
Sodium Points 2
Fiber Points 0
Carbohydrate Points 0
Cholesterol Points 5

Roasted Chicken with Rosemary

Serves: 4-6
Preparation Time: 1 hour 20 minutes

1   whole chicken
3   sprigs fresh rosemary
¼   cup (60 ml) olive oil

Clean chicken, place whole sprig of rosemary in cavity and one in fold of each wing next to breast (tie chicken with string to keep rosemary in place). Baste chicken with olive oil. Place chicken on its side in 6-quart (6 L) roaster. Cover and cook over low heat 30 minutes. Turn to other side and cook additional 30 minutes, then cook upright the last 20 minutes. Serve with rice.

If desired deglaze pan using chicken broth or white wine, thicken slightly with cornstarch and water. Serve as sauce for chicken or rice.

NUTRITIONAL BREAKDOWN
PER SERVING:
Calories 364
Fat Grams 25
Carbohydrate Grams 2
Protein Grams 31
Cholesterol mg 121
Sodium mg 84
THE POINT SYSTEM
Calorie Points 5
Protein Points 4
Fat Grams 25
Sodium Points 4
Fiber Points 0
Carbohydrate Points 0
Cholesterol Points 12

CHICKEN

3   breasts, skinned
3   legs and thighs, skinned

MARINADE

1   teaspoon paprika
½   teaspoon cayenne pepper
1   teaspoon sugar
1   teaspoon pepper, freshly ground
1   teaspoon cumin, freshly ground
1   teaspoon coriander, freshly ground
3   cloves fresh garlic, minced
1   teaspoon ginger, freshly grated
3   tablespoons vinegar
2   tablespoons tomato ketchup
2   tablespoons olive oil

Chicken Tikka

Serves: 6
Preparation Time: 15 minutes
(Marinate: 2 hours)

Score chicken with sharp knife through to bone every ½ inch (1.5 cm). In large bowl mix together the marinade ingredients, add scored chicken to marinade, cover and refrigerate 2-24 hours.

Preheat large frypan over medium heat until drops of water "dance" when sprinkled in pan.

Place chicken, meat side down, in pan. Be careful of placement as initially chicken will stick. When chicken releases after approximately 5 minutes, turn, cover and cook other side additional 5-7 minutes. Scoring the chicken allows it to cook quickly.

SAUCE

In small saucepan heat remaining marinade for an additional 5 minutes. Pour over cooked chicken on platter.

NUTRITIONAL BREAKDOWN
PER SERVING:
Calories 286
Fat Grams 12
Carbohydrate Grams 3
Protein Grams 40
Cholesterol mg 118
Sodium mg 141
THE POINT SYSTEM
Calorie Points 4
Protein Points 5
Fat Grams 12
Sodium Points 6
Fiber Points 0
Carbohydrate Points 0
Cholesterol Points 12

Chicken Satay with Peanut Sauce

Serves: 8
Preparation Time: 1 hour 15 minutes

1	package (16) bamboo skewers
1½	teaspoons fennel seed
2	teaspoons ground turmeric
2	pounds (1 kg) boneless chicken breast
¾	cup (180 ml) unsweetened coconut milk
1	tablespoon soy sauce

Soak skewers in water 10 minutes. Meanwhile dry roast fennel seeds in 8" chef pan until light brown. Grind turmeric and fennel together with mortar and pestle or in coffee grinder used for herbs. Slice chicken into ½" (1.5 cm) wide strips, the length of the breast. Ribbon thread chicken strips onto 16 skewers, place in deep bowl.

Combine coconut milk, soy sauce and ground spices. Pour over skewers in bowl stirring to coat. Marinate 1 hour in refrigerator.

Preheat 13" (33 cm) chef pan until water drops "dance" across pan. Place chicken on skewers in pan, turn as they release from pan — about 3 minutes each side. Skewers may be cooked over open flame (grill or broiler) or deep fried in hot wok.

½	cup peanut butter
¼	cup (60 ml) warm water
⅓	cup (80 ml) rice wine vinegar
1	clove garlic, minced
½	tablespoon ginger, chopped
1	teaspoon sugar
1	teaspoon red chili flakes
¼	cup (60 ml) sesame oil

Peanut Sauce

Yields: 1½ cups
Serving size: 1 tablespoon
Preparation Time: 15 minutes

Thin peanut butter by stirring in warm water slowly using a wire whisk. Whisk in all other ingredients except sesame oil. Slowly blend in sesame oil by pouring a very thin stream of oil as you continue to whisk peanut sauce.

NUTRITIONAL BREAKDOWN
PER SERVING:
CHICKEN SATAY
Calories 340
Fat Grams 12
Carbohydrate Grams 2
Protein Grams 54
Cholesterol mg 146
Sodium mg 259
THE POINT SYSTEM
Calorie Points 5
Protein Points 7
Fat Grams 12
Sodium Points 11
Fiber Points 0
Carbohydrate Points 0
Cholesterol Points 15

NUTRITIONAL BREAKDOWN
PER SERVING:
PEANUT SAUCE
Calories 36
Fat Grams 3
Carbohydrate Grams 2
Protein Grams 1
Cholesterol mg 0
Sodium mg 31
THE POINT SYSTEM
Calorie Points 1/2
Protein Points 2
Fat Grams 3
Sodium Points 1 1/2
Fiber Points 0
Carbohydrate Points 0
Cholesterol Points 0

Ground Turkey Stuffed Peppers

Serves: 6
Preparation Time: 1 hour

1½ cups (360 ml) chicken broth
¾ cup rice
1 tablespoon olive oil
1 onion, chopped
2 cloves garlic, minced
1½ pounds (700 g) ground turkey
1 32 ounce (910 g) can tomato sauce
4 tablespoons fresh parsley, chopped
1 teaspoon salt
½ teaspoon fresh ground pepper
6 large green bell peppers

In 2-quart saucepan (2 L utensil) bring chicken broth to boil. Add rice, stir, cover and remove from heat.

In large frypan over medium heat sauté onion and garlic in olive oil 3-5 minutes. Add ground turkey, cook until turkey is no longer pink. Remove from heat and drain fat.

Add rice, sauce, parsley, salt and pepper to turkey. Stir together. Cut tops off bell peppers and seed. Stuff each pepper with turkey-rice mixture. Stand stuffed pepper upright in 6-quart (6 L) utensil. Spoon remaining sauce on top of peppers, add 3 tablespoons water to bottom of pan. Cover and cook over medium heat 10 minutes, reduce to low for 30 minutes.

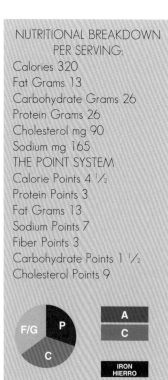

NUTRITIONAL BREAKDOWN
PER SERVING:
Calories 320
Fat Grams 13
Carbohydrate Grams 26
Protein Grams 26
Cholesterol mg 90
Sodium mg 165
THE POINT SYSTEM
Calorie Points 4 ½
Protein Points 3
Fat Grams 13
Sodium Points 7
Fiber Points 3
Carbohydrate Points 1 ½
Cholesterol Points 9

2	whole chicken breasts
	water
1	onion cut in half
1	bay leaf
8	peppercorns
	salt to taste
3	tablespoons Parmesan cheese (reduced calorie)
½	cup Monterey Jack cheese
1	4.5 ounce (125 g) can green chilies
1	15 ounce (425 g) can tomatoes, drained
¼	cup cilantro
½	cup (120 ml) buttermilk
8	corn tortillas
½	cup cheddar cheese

Chicken Enchiladas

Serves: 8
Preparation Time: 1 hour

Place chicken breast (in water just to cover), ½ onion, bay leaf and peppercorns in 2-quart saucepan (2 L utensil). Cover and cook over low heat 30 minutes. Keeping chicken in broth, cool (reserve broth in freezer for future use). Shred chicken and mix in cheeses. In blender combine green chilies, tomatoes, cilantro and buttermilk; set aside. To soften tortillas place between damp paper towels in 8" chef pan, cover and place over low heat for 10 minutes. Fill each tortilla with one-eighth of the mixture and roll tightly. Place in 13" (33 cm) chef pan, seam side down. Pour reserved tomato chili mixture over top. Sprinkle top with cheddar cheese. Cover and cook over medium to low heat 25 minutes. Serve with shredded lettuce, non-fat sour cream and chopped olives, if desired.

Note: Low fat and non-fat cheeses do not melt as well. Use non-fat cheeses in combination with whole fat cheese or in dishes such as this that contain plenty of moisture.

NUTRITIONAL BREAKDOWN
PER SERVING:
Calories 202
Fat Grams 5
Carbohydrate Grams 18
Protein Grams 22
Cholesterol mg 44
Sodium mg 250
THE POINT SYSTEM
Calorie Points 2½
Protein Points 3
Fat Grams 5
Sodium Points 11
Fiber Points 1
Carbohydrate Points 1
Cholesterol Points 4

Teriyaki Chicken

Serves: 4
Preparation Time: 1 hour 15 minutes

2	chicken breasts, boned
¼	cup brown sugar
¼	cup (60 ml) rice wine vinegar
2	tablespoons soy sauce
1	tablespoon ginger, grated
1	clove garlic, minced
1	onion, sliced
1	green pepper, sliced
1	red pepper, sliced
1	cup fresh pineapple

Slice chicken into ½" (1.5 cm) strips. Mix together brown sugar, vinegar, soy sauce, ginger, and garlic. Marinate chicken ½ hour.

Preheat wok or large frypan over medium-high heat, add chicken strips, stir-fry 2 minutes, add onion, peppers, and pineapple. Add marinade, toss, cover and cook 5 minutes. Serve over rice or rice noodles.

NUTRITIONAL BREAKDOWN
PER SERVING:
Calories 259
Fat Grams 4
Carbohydrate Grams 28
Protein Grams 29
Cholesterol mg 73
Sodium mg 587
THE POINT SYSTEM
Calorie Points 3½
Protein Points 4
Fat Grams 4
Sodium Points 26
Fiber Points 1
Carbohydrate Points 2
Cholesterol Points 7

1	turkey breast, skinless, cut into strips
1	onion, sliced thin
3	cloves garlic, chopped
1	16 ounce (460 g) can chopped tomatoes
1½	cups dried orzo
2	cups (480 ml) water
1	cup broccoli florets

Turkey with Orzo and Broccoli

Serves: 8
Preparation Time: 30 minutes

Preheat 13" (33 cm) electric pan or chef pan over medium heat. Place turkey in pan, cover (vent open). Turn turkey after 5 minutes, brown second side. Reduce heat to 275°F (135°C) or low setting. Add onion and garlic, sauté 2 minutes. Add tomatoes and mix well; push mixture to center of pan. Pour dried orzo around outside of pan, pour water over orzo, cover (vent closed) 5 minutes; add broccoli to top, cover for an additional 5 minutes. Serve directly from pan.

NUTRITIONAL BREAKDOWN
PER SERVING
Calories 165
Fat Grams 1
Carbohydrate Grams 14
Protein Grams 25
Cholesterol mg 64
Sodium mg 137
THE POINT SYSTEM
Calorie Points 2
Protein Points 3
Fat Grams 1
Sodium Points 6
Fiber Points 0
Carbohydrate Points 1
Cholesterol Points 6

Apple-Chicken Rolls

Serves: 4
Preparation Time: 1 hour

¼	cup green onions, finely chopped
1	cup (240 ml) unsweetened apple juice, divided
½	cup peeled apple, finely chopped
½	cup soft rye bread crumbs
2	tablespoons fresh parsley, minced
⅛	teaspoon caraway seeds
4	4-ounce (115 g) boned chicken breast halves, skinned
2	tablespoons brandy
1	tablespoon cornstarch
	apple slices (optional)

In large frypan cook onions covered over medium heat 10 minutes or until tender. Remove from heat. Stir in 2 tablespoons apple juice, chopped apple, bread crumbs, parsley, and caraway seeds. Remove from pan, and set aside.

Place chicken between 2 sheets of wax paper; flatten to ¼" (75 mm) thickness, using a meat mallet or rolling pin. Divide bread crumb mixture evenly among chicken breast halves, spooning mixture into center of each half. Roll breast up lengthwise, tucking ends under. Secure with wooden picks. Preheat large frypan.

Brown chicken on all sides over medium heat uncovered (approximately 15 minutes). Add 2 tablespoons apple juice and brandy. Cover, reduce heat, and simmer 30 minutes, or until chicken is tender. Transfer chicken to a serving platter; remove wooden picks, and keep warm (or slice Apple-Chicken Rolls and arrange them to show off the spiral apple filling).

Add cornstarch to pan juices in frypan; stir until smooth. Stir in remaining ¾ cup apple juice. Bring to a boil; cook 1 minute or until thickened and bubbly. Spoon sauce over chicken rolls. Garnish with apple slices, if desired. Serve with couscous cooked in water with lemon, 1 teaspoon butter and sliced apples.

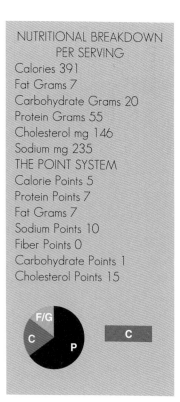

NUTRITIONAL BREAKDOWN
PER SERVING
Calories 391
Fat Grams 7
Carbohydrate Grams 20
Protein Grams 55
Cholesterol mg 146
Sodium mg 235
THE POINT SYSTEM
Calorie Points 5
Protein Points 7
Fat Grams 7
Sodium Points 10
Fiber Points 0
Carbohydrate Points 1
Cholesterol Points 15

113

Fish & Seafood.

Orange Roughy á la Asparagus

Serves: 8
Preparation Time: 25 minutes

1   pound (460 g) fresh asparagus spears
1   2 ounce (60 g) jar pimientos, diced and drained
2   tablespoons lemon juice
¼   teaspoon dried whole thyme
⅛   teaspoon garlic powder
⅛   teaspoon pepper
3   pounds (1.4 kg) orange roughy fillets
2   tablespoons sliced almonds

Cut asparagus into 1" (2.5 cm) pieces. Combine asparagus with pimiento, lemon juice, thyme, garlic powder, and pepper; set aside.

Arrange fillets in a 13" (33 cm) chef pan. Spoon asparagus mixture over fillets. Cover and cook over medium heat 20 minutes or until fish flakes easily when tested with fork. Sprinkle with almonds.

NUTRITIONAL BREAKDOWN
PER SERVING
Calories 149
Fat Grams 2
Carbohydrate Grams 2
Protein Grams 29
Cholesterol mg 35
Sodium mg 178
THE POINT SYSTEM
Calorie Points 2
Protein Points 4
Fat Grams 2
Sodium Points 8
Fiber Points 1
Carbohydrate Points 0
Cholesterol Points 4

Scallops with Chives and Peppers

Serves: 4
Preparation Time: 15 minutes

½	tablespoon olive oil
1	tablespoon low-calorie margarine
2	hot chili peppers, dried (optional)
¾	pound (360 g) fresh scallops
3	tablespoons fresh chives, chopped
½	red pepper, chopped
	pinch ground cloves or cinnamon

Heat oil and margarine in large frypan. Add chili peppers and sauté for 30 seconds. Add scallops and sauté just long enough to heat through, about 2 minutes. Stir in chives, red pepper, and cloves. Cook for 30 seconds more. Serve over pasta or rice.

NUTRITIONAL BREAKDOWN
PER SERVING:
Calories 138
Fat Grams 5
Carbohydrate Grams 4
Protein Grams 21
Cholesterol mg 45
Sodium mg 261
THE POINT SYSTEM
Calorie Points 2
Protein Points 3
Fat Grams 5
Sodium Points 11
Fiber Points 1
Carbohydrate Points ½
Cholesterol Points 5

F/G
C
P
A
C
IRON
HIERRO

Spinach Fish Rolls

Serves: 6
Preparation Time: 40 minutes

½	bag frozen spinach, chopped
½	cup feta cheese
½	cup low fat cottage cheese
2	teaspoons lemon zest
1	egg
1	small onion, chopped
3	cloves garlic, minced
1	teaspoon oregano
6	thin fish fillets (sole)
1	lemon

Partially thaw the finely chopped spinach, squeeze excess water from spinach. Mix chopped spinach and all other ingredients except lemon and fish.

Place ¼ cup of filling mixture in middle of each fish portion. Starting with the narrow end of fillet, roll fish over filling. Place seam side down in large frypan. Cover, cook over low to medium heat for 30 minutes.

Variation
Italian Fish Rolls

Serves: 8
Preparation Time: 40 minutes

1	9 ounce (260 g) bag frozen, French-style green beans
2	tablespoons onion, chopped
1	8 ounce (230 g) can tomato sauce
¼	teaspoon oregano leaves
¼	teaspoon basil leaves
⅛	teaspoon garlic powder
1	tablespoon Parmesan cheese, grated
8	flounder fillets without skin

Place onions and frozen beans in 2-quart saucepan (2 L utensil), cover and cook over medium heat 5 minutes; reduce heat to low for additional 5 minutes. Remove from heat.

In separate bowl, mix together tomato sauce, oregano, basil, garlic powder, and Parmesan cheese. Fill fillets with bean mixture as above, place in pan, and pour prepared sauce over top of fish rolls. Cover and cook at low to medium heat for 30 minutes.

NUTRITIONAL BREAKDOWN PER SERVING:	NUTRITIONAL BREAKDOWN PER SERVING:
SPINACH FISH ROLLS	**ITALIAN FISH ROLLS**
Calories 257	Calories 260
Fat Grams 6	Fat Grams 3
Carbohydrate Grams 10	Carbohydrate Grams 4
Protein Grams 40	Protein Grams 51
Cholesterol mg 104	Cholesterol mg 96
Sodium mg 518	Sodium mg 297
THE POINT SYSTEM	THE POINT SYSTEM
Calorie Points 3 1/2	Calorie Points 3 1/2
Protein Points 5	Protein Points 6
Fat Grams 6	Fat Grams 3
Sodium Points 23	Sodium Points 13
Fiber Points 1	Fiber Points 0
Carbohydrate Points 1/2	Carbohydrate Points 1/2
Cholesterol Points 10	Cholesterol Points 9 1/2

Catfish Barbecue

Serves: 6
Preparation Time: 50 minutes

⅓   cup (80 ml) reduced calorie ketchup
1   tablespoon lemon juice
1   teaspoon brown sugar
2   teaspoons vegetable oil
1   teaspoon low-sodium Worcestershire sauce
½   teaspoon dried whole marjoram
¼   teaspoon garlic powder
¼   teaspoon ground red pepper
6   4 ounce (120 g) farm-raised catfish fillets

Combine ketchup, lemon juice, brown sugar, vegetable oil, Worcestershire sauce, marjoram, garlic powder, and red pepper in a small bowl. Arrange fillets in dish. Pour ketchup mixture over fillets; cover and marinate in refrigerator 30 minutes, turning once. Remove fillets from marinade, reserving marinade. Bring marinade to a boil in 1-quart saucepan (1.5 L utensil); boil 2 minutes. Warm 10" chef pan or large frypan over medium heat. Place fillets in warm pan. Cover and cook 15 minutes or until fish flakes easily when tested with a fork. Remove to serving platter. Pour warm marinade over fillets.

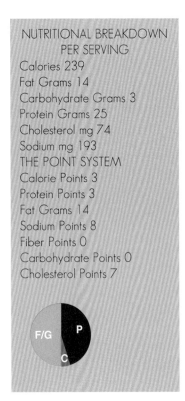

NUTRITIONAL BREAKDOWN
PER SERVING
Calories 239
Fat Grams 14
Carbohydrate Grams 3
Protein Grams 25
Cholesterol mg 74
Sodium mg 193
THE POINT SYSTEM
Calorie Points 3
Protein Points 3
Fat Grams 14
Sodium Points 8
Fiber Points 0
Carbohydrate Points 0
Cholesterol Points 7

1	medium onion, chopped
1	large green pepper, chopped
½	cup celery, chopped
1	clove garlic, minced
1	32 ounce (920 g) can stewed tomatoes *or* 4 fresh tomatoes, quartered
1	cup (240 ml) water
1	cup long grain rice, uncooked
1	bay leaf
½	teaspoon dried thyme
1	teaspoon dried basil
¼	teaspoon red pepper
1	12 ounce (340 g) package frozen shrimp, thawed
½	pound (230 g) bay scallops

Scallop Shrimp Jambalaya

Serves: 8
Preparation Time: 40 minutes

In 13" (33 cm) chef pan sauté onions, green pepper, celery and garlic over medium heat 10 minutes or until tender.

Add stewed tomatoes, water, rice, bay leaf, dried thyme, basil and red pepper. Stir. Cover and simmer over low heat 15 minutes. Add shrimp and scallops. Simmer another 5-10 minutes or until scallops are opaque.

Serve with hot sauce.

NUTRITIONAL BREAKDOWN
PER SERVING
Calories 175
Fat Grams 1
Carbohydrate Grams 24
Protein Grams 18
Cholesterol mg 79
Sodium mg 783
THE POINT SYSTEM
Calorie Points 2½
Protein Points 2
Fat Grams 1
Sodium Points 34
Fiber Points 2
Carbohydrate Points 1½
Cholesterol Points 8

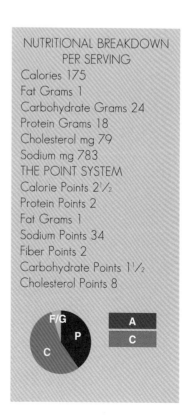

Steamed Mussels

1	tablespoon olive oil
2	medium onions, minced
4	cloves garlic, minced
2	cups (480 ml) red wine
48	fresh mussels*

In a 6-quart (6 L) roaster, sauté onions and garlic in olive oil until tender, add wine and bring to a boil. Add mussels, cover, lower heat to medium-low for 5-7 minutes or until mussels open. Serve in soup bowls with wine mixture and toasted French bread.

*Mussels need to breathe. Remove from bag as soon as possible and soak in fresh water. To clean mussels prior to cooking, soak in cold water with 4 tablespoons cornstarch for 30 minutes. Scrape beards off, rinse and soak again in fresh cold water. Discard any mussels that are open before cooking. Do not eat mussels that do not open after cooking.

Serves: 8
Preparation Time: 40 minutes

NUTRITIONAL BREAKDOWN
PER SERVING:
Calories 190
Fat Grams 4
Carbohydrate Grams 10
Protein Grams 17
Cholesterol mg 63
Sodium mg 364
THE POINT SYSTEM
Calorie Points 3
Protein Points 2
Fat Grams 4
Sodium Points 16
Fiber Points ½
Carbohydrate Points 1
Cholesterol Points 6

Variation
Mussels in Tomato Broth

Use white wine instead of red. Add:

1	32 ounce (920 g) can plum tomatoes, chopped
1	cup flat-leaf parsley, chopped
2	teaspoons dried oregano

Simmer 15 minutes before adding mussels.

Nutritional breakdown not included for this variation.

2	tablespoons vegetable oil
3	tablespoons red curry paste
1½	pounds (700 g) medium shrimp, peeled and drained
1	whole fresh pineapple, cubed
1	cup (240 ml) coconut milk, unsweetened
2	tablespoons sugar
½	teaspoon fennel seeds, ground
1	teaspoon turmeric
1	tablespoon lime zest
¼	cup (60 ml) low sodium soy sauce

Thai Red Curry Shrimp and Pineapple

Serves: 8
Preparation Time: 20 minutes

Warm vegetable oil in wok or large frypan over medium-high heat until hot. Add red curry paste stirring to separate paste. Stir in shrimp, cook approximately 3 minutes. Stir in pineapple, then add remaining ingredients, simmer 5-6 minutes.

Serve over prepared jasmine rice, garnish with cilantro and roasted peanuts.

NUTRITIONAL BREAKDOWN
PER SERVING:
Calories 187
Fat Grams 9
Carbohydrate Grams 14
Protein Grams 15
Cholesterol mg 102
Sodium mg 800
THE POINT SYSTEM
Calorie Points 2½
Protein Points 2
Fat Grams 9
Sodium Points 35
Fiber Points 1
Carbohydrate Points 1
Cholesterol Points 10

Paella

Serves: 16
Preparation Time: 45 minutes

2	tablespoons olive oil
2	pounds (1 kg) chicken wings
1	pound (460 g) chorizo
¼	pound (120 g) lean pork, diced
¼	pound (120 g) ham, diced
4	cloves garlic
3	onions, chopped
2	green peppers, chopped
3	fresh tomatoes, quartered then halved
1	teaspoon oregano
5	cups (1.25 L) water
½	teaspoon salt
¼	teaspoon pepper
2	cups raw rice
¼	teaspoon saffron
1	pound (460 g) cooked shrimp
½	pound (230 g) cooked lobster, chunked
1	10 ounce (300 g) package frozen peas
1	32 ounce (920 g) can artichoke hearts
1	4 ounce (120 g) can pimientos, sliced
12	clams or mussels, steamed separately

In 13" (33 cm) chef pan brown chicken, chorizo, pork, and ham in olive oil over medium-high heat. Add garlic, onion, then green pepper, tomato and oregano. Add water, salt, pepper, rice and saffron, cover, reduce heat to medium 15 minutes. Add shrimp, lobster, peas and artichoke hearts, turn from bottom. Cover and cook an additional 10 minutes. Garnish top with pimiento, mussels and/or clams.

NUTRITIONAL BREAKDOWN
PER SERVING:
Calories 341
Fat Grams 16
Carbohydrate Grams 25
Protein Grams 26
Cholesterol mg 96
Sodium mg 656
THE POINT SYSTEM
Calorie Points 4½
Protein Points 3
Fat Grams 16
Sodium Points 29
Fiber Points 3
Carbohydrate Points 1½
Cholesterol Points 10

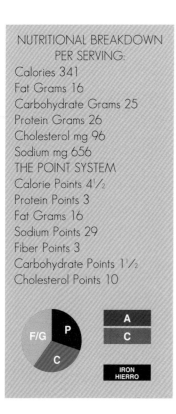

In Spain there are hundreds of "authentic" recipes for Paella, for into this colorful melange of rice, seafood, meat, and chicken, anything can go. It can be made with seafood only; or with meat only; or only with chicken and chicken livers. The green vegetable added may be peas, snap beans, limas or artichoke hearts. The meat used may be pork, veal, or ham. Into a family Paella, for that matter, any bits of leftovers may be added.

Despite this broad umbrella, certain basic rules are important. The dish must always be made with olive oil, which helps to brown the chicken and meat evenly and to keep each grain of rice separate. Saffron must always be added, to give the rice its golden color and the sauce its special pungency.

Shrimp
Spring Rolls

Serves: 8
Preparation Time: 30 minutes

½	cup dried black mushrooms (shitake or wood ear) spring roll wrappers*
3	tablespoons peanut oil
1	pound (460 g) shrimp, peeled, cleaned and chopped
3	shallots, minced
1	garlic clove
1	tablespoon ginger, minced
1	celery rib, minced
1	serrano chili, minced
1	carrot, minced
½	pound (230 g) bean sprouts
1	tablespoon soy sauce
1	teaspoon sesame oil
1	tablespoon sake or dry sherry
½	teaspoon 5-spice mix**
2	teaspoons cornstarch
½	cup (120 ml) water
1	tablespoon cornstarch

*Spring roll wrappers available frozen or at Oriental markets

**See 5-Spice Mix in the Spice section, page 201.

Soak dried mushrooms in hot water 10 minutes, drain, squeeze dry and chop. Heat oil in wok or large frypan, stir fry shrimp for 30 seconds. Add all vegetables adding bean sprouts last. Mix all seasonings together with 2 teaspoons cornstarch. Add to wok and toss to combine. Immediately spread mixture onto cookie sheet to cool.

Mix together water and 1 tablespoon cornstarch to seal edges. "Burrito" roll each wrapper by placing approximately 2 tablespoons of filling one-third the way up the wrapper. Fold corner over filling forming lightly packed log shaped roll. Fold side edges over and roll to end of wrapper. Seal edges with cornstarch and water mixture and finish rolling. Repeat with other wrappers.

Heat 2" (5 cm) of oil in wok or large frypan to 375°F (190°C). Fry 2-3 spring rolls at a time until golden brown. Drain and serve with soy dipping sauce.

NUTRITIONAL BREAKDOWN
PER SERVING:
Calories 117
Fat Grams 2
Carbohydrate Grams 9
Protein Grams 14
Cholesterol mg 85
Sodium mg 563
THE POINT SYSTEM
Calorie Points 2
Protein Points 2
Fat Grams 2
Sodium Points 24
Fiber Points 1
Carbohydrate Points ½
Cholesterol Points 8

Soy Dipping Sauce

Yields: 2 cups (480 ml)
Preparation Time: 10 minutes

½	cup (120 ml) water
½	cup (120 ml) white vinegar
½	cup (120 ml) soy sauce
½	cup sugar
1	teaspoon ground chili paste
2	teaspoons garlic, chopped

Mix all ingredients in small bowl.

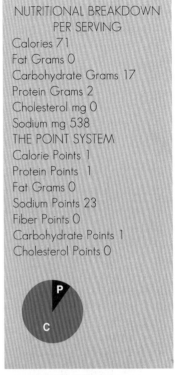

NUTRITIONAL BREAKDOWN
PER SERVING
Calories 71
Fat Grams 0
Carbohydrate Grams 17
Protein Grams 2
Cholesterol mg 0
Sodium mg 538
THE POINT SYSTEM
Calorie Points 1
Protein Points 1
Fat Grams 0
Sodium Points 23
Fiber Points 0
Carbohydrate Points 1
Cholesterol Points 0

Poached Salmon

Serves: 6
Preparation Time: 35 minutes

4	cups (1 L) water
½	cup onion, chopped
½	cup carrots, chopped
½	cup celery, chopped
2	cloves garlic, minced
6	peppercorns
4	whole allspice
1	teaspoon bouquet garni*
2	tablespoons lemon juice
1	pound (460 g) salmon fillet

In 4-quart (4 L) utensil combine all of the ingredients except the fish. Bring to a boil, then reduce to simmer for 20 minutes. Place fillet in simmering liquid, cover and simmer until done, approximately 15 minutes. Remove with large spatula. Serve with fresh vegetables.

*See Bouquet Garni in the Spice section, page 201.

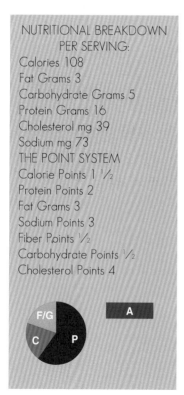

NUTRITIONAL BREAKDOWN
PER SERVING:
Calories 108
Fat Grams 3
Carbohydrate Grams 5
Protein Grams 16
Cholesterol mg 39
Sodium mg 73
THE POINT SYSTEM
Calorie Points 1 ½
Protein Points 2
Fat Grams 3
Sodium Points 3
Fiber Points ½
Carbohydrate Points ½
Cholesterol Points 4

6	slices canned pineapple
1	tablespoon olive oil
⅔	cup (160 ml) pineapple juice
2	large green peppers cut into 1" (2.5 cm) pieces
2	tablespoons cornstarch
2	teaspoons low sodium soy sauce
2	tablespoons vinegar
3	tablespoons sugar
1	cup (240 ml) low sodium chicken broth
1	14 ounce (400 g) can water-packed tuna salt and pepper to taste
4-6	cups cooked rice or crisp noodles

In 13" (33 cm) chef pan sauté pineapple in olive oil for 5 minutes. Add ⅓ cup pineapple juice and green pepper. Cover and simmer 10 minutes. Mix cornstarch with remaining pineapple juice, add to pan with soy sauce, vinegar, sugar and chicken broth. Cook and stir until thickened. Add tuna, salt and pepper. Heat through. Serve over crisp Chinese noodles or rice.

Sweet and Sour Tuna

Serves: 8
Preparation Time: 15 minutes

NUTRITIONAL BREAKDOWN
PER SERVING:
Calories 206
Fat Grams 3
Carbohydrate Grams 30
Protein Grams 15
Cholesterol mg 15
Sodium mg 224
THE POINT SYSTEM
Calorie Points 2 ½
Protein Points 2
Fat Grams 3
Sodium Points 10
Fiber Points 0
Carbohydrate Points 2
Cholesterol Points 1

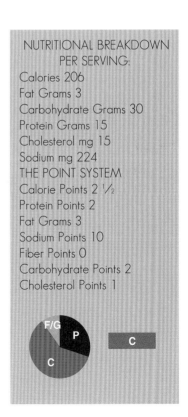

Seafood Filé Gumbo

Serves: 6
Preparation Time: 50 minutes

5   cups (1.25 L) water
    shellfish boil spice
6   crayfish
½   pound (230 g) pork shoulder, cubed
2   tablespoons low calorie margarine
1   onion, sliced
1   green pepper, sliced
2   cloves garlic, chopped
3   tablespoons flour
½   teaspoon thyme
1   bay leaf
2   tablespoons parsley, chopped
½   teaspoon Worcestershire sauce
12 oysters (frozen)
1   pound (460 g) cooked shrimp
8   tomatoes chopped
2   cups sliced okra
    salt and pepper
2   tablespoons filé powder
    cooked rice

Peel shrimp. Bring water to boil in 3-quart saucepan (3 L utensil), add spice mixture, and crayfish. Simmer 15 minutes. Meanwhile preheat 6-quart (6 L) roaster over medium-high heat. Brown pork cubes on all sides, remove to platter. Reduce heat to medium-low, melt butter, add onion, green pepper, garlic, and flour. Stir constantly until flour is pale golden brown. Gradually strain stock from spice mixture into roaster. Add thyme and bay leaf, stir well. Add parsley, Worcestershire sauce, oysters, shrimp, crayfish, reserved pork, and tomatoes, heat through. Stir in okra and filé. Adjust seasoning and serve over rice.

NUTRITIONAL BREAKDOWN
PER SERVING:
Calories 432
Fat Grams 8
Carbohydrate Grams 52
Protein Grams 39
Cholesterol mg 159
Sodium mg 732
THE POINT SYSTEM
Calorie Points 6
Protein Points 5
Fat Grams 8
Sodium Points 32
Fiber Points 1
Carbohydrate Points 3½
Cholesterol Points 16

F/G P C

A
C
CALCIUM
CALCIO
IRON
HIERRO

1	pound (460 g) halibut fillets*
1	egg white
1	tablespoon cornstarch
2	teaspoons white wine
	salt and pepper
	peanut oil for frying
1	large onion, 1/2" (1.5 cm) thick wedges
1	tablespoon curry powder
2	teaspoons sugar (optional)
1	20 ounce (570 g) can pineapple pieces (reserve juice) or 1/2 fresh pineapple cubed
1	11 ounce (310 g) can mandarin oranges (reserve juice)
1	8 ounce (230 g) can water chestnuts, drained
1	tablespoon cornstarch mixed with juice of
1	lime

Singapore Fish

Serves: 6
Preparation Time: 30 minutes

Skin fillets and cut into even sized pieces, about 2" (5 cm) each. Mix together egg white, cornstarch, wine, salt and pepper. Place fish in mixture, stir to coat. Heat oil in wok or large frypan over medium high heat. When hot, add a few pieces of fish at a time, fry until golden brown, drain on paper towels. Continue with remaining fish. Remove oil from wok, add onion, stir-fry 1-2 minutes, add curry powder, cook an additional 1-2 minutes. Add reserved juices, bring to boil. Combine lime juice and cornstarch, stir into boiling juices. Add sugar, fruit, water chestnuts, and fried fish to wok, stir to coat. Heat through 1 minute. Serve immediately.

*Chicken may be substituted for fish.

NUTRITIONAL BREAKDOWN
PER SERVING:
Calories 250
Fat Grams 11
Carbohydrate Grams 21
Protein Grams 17
Cholesterol mg 24
Sodium mg 58
THE POINT SYSTEM
Calorie Points 3 1/2
Protein Points 2
Fat Grams 11
Sodium Points 2 1/2
Fiber Points 1
Carbohydrate Points 1 1/2
Cholesterol Points 2

Eggs & Cheese

Strawberry Cheese Blintzes

Yields: 12 ❖ Serves: 6
Preparation Time: 20 minutes

❖　　❖　　❖

1½　cups non-fat cottage cheese
½　　cup light cream cheese
2　　egg whites, lightly beaten
2　　tablespoon honey
1　　teaspoon grated lemon zest
½　　teaspoon vanilla
12　basic crêpes (recipe below)
⅓　　cup Frozen Strawberry Jam, thawed*
⅓　　cup non-fat sour cream

In large bowl, combine cottage cheese, cream cheese, egg whites, honey, lemon zest and vanilla. Spoon 3 tablespoons cheese mixture into center of each crêpe. Fold right and left sides of crêpe over filling, forming a square. Place blintzes seam side down in 13" (33 cm) chef pan. Cover. Place chef pan over medium-low heat for 10 minutes or until blintzes are thoroughly heated. Top evenly with strawberry jam, then cover with sour cream.

*See recipe for Frozen Strawberry Jam, page 139.

NUTRITIONAL BREAKDOWN PER SERVING
(includes crêpes)

Calories 132
Fat Grams 4
Carbohydrate Grams 17
Protein Grams 8
Cholesterol mg 4
Sodium mg 290
THE POINT SYSTEM
Calorie Points 2
Protein Points 1
Fat Grams 4
Sodium Points 13
Fiber Points 0
Carbohydrate Points 1
Cholesterol Points 0

Basic Crêpes
Yields: 6 portions
Preparation Time: 30 minutes

1　　cup sifted flour
½　　teaspoon salt
3　　eggs, well beaten
1　　cup (240 ml) milk
2　　tablespoons shortening, melted

Mix flour and salt. Combine eggs and milk; add flour and beat until smooth. Add shortening. Heat 8" chef pan or small frypan until water drops "dance" when sprinkled in pan. Grease pan lightly but thoroughly. Pour in 2 tablespoons batter. Lift pan off heat and tilt from side to side until batter covers bottom evenly. Return to heat; cook until underside is lightly browned. To remove, slide crêpe out of pan onto plate. Cook one crêpe at a time.

1   12 ounce (340 g) box of jumbo shells

FILLING

2   pounds (1 kg) ricotta cheese, low-fat
1   cup mozzarella, shredded
⅓   cup Romano, grated
½   teaspoon black pepper
3   eggs
1   10 ounce (300 g) package frozen chopped
    spinach, thawed and drained
3   cups Marinara Sauce*
    Parmesan cheese

In pasta pan or 6-quart (6 L) utensil, bring 4 quarts (4 L) water to strong boil, add 1/2 teaspoon salt. Empty package of shells into center insert basket. Bring back to boil, stir-frequently to separate shells; cook only 8-10 minutes. Shells should still feel firm.

Remove insert; rinse shells under cold water to stop cooking process, drain and set aside.

Mix all of filling ingredients. Cover the bottom of 13" (33 cm) chef pan with 1 cup marinara sauce. Fill each shell with approximately 1 tablespoon filling and place seam side down in sauce coated pan. Cover filled shells with marinara sauce. Serve with low-fat or non-fat Parmesan cheese. Cover pan; cook over medium to low heat 25 minutes.

* Marinara sauce is not included in nutritional breakdown. See recipe on page 149.

Spinach Cheese Jumbo Shells

Serves: 10
Preparation Time: 50 minutes

NUTRITIONAL BREAKDOWN
PER SERVING
Calories 291
Fat Grams 10
Carbohydrate Grams 25
Protein Grams 23
Cholesterol mg 24
Sodium mg 704
THE POINT SYSTEM
Calorie Points 4
Protein Points 3
Fat Grams 10
Sodium Points 31
Fiber Points 1
Carbohydrate Points 1½
Cholesterol Points 2

Mardi Gras Family Omelet

Serves: 10
Preparation Time: 30 minutes

½	pound (230 g) ground sausage
1	tablespoon beef broth
½	green pepper, sliced
½	red pepper, sliced
½	yellow pepper, sliced
6	mushrooms, sliced
8	eggs or equivalent egg substitutes*
2	tablespoons skim milk
3	tablespoons butter
2	tomatoes, sliced
½	cup Monterey Jack cheese, grated
½	cup cheddar cheese, grated
¼	cup green onion

Brown sausage in 10" chef pan or large frypan over medium -high heat. Drain sausage on paper towels. In 13" (33 cm) chef pan sauté peppers and mushrooms in beef broth over medium heat until softened, remove to side dish. Beat eggs or egg substitutes in bowl with milk. Melt butter in chef pan over medium heat, add beaten egg mixture, cover and cook 10 minutes or until eggs are almost set. Add reserved peppers and mushrooms, tomatoes, and half of the cheese on one side of omelet. Flip omelet with spatula over vegetables; top omelet with remaining cheese and green onion. Cover, reduce to low, cook additional 5 minutes. Serve from chef pan, or slide onto oval platter.

* Nutritional breakdown uses egg substitutes.

NUTRITIONAL BREAKDOWN
PER SERVING
Calories 216
Fat Grams 15
Carbohydrate Grams 6
Protein Grams 13
Cholesterol mg 44
Sodium mg 631
THE POINT SYSTEM
Calorie Points 3
Protein Points 2
Fat Grams 15
Sodium Points 27
Fiber Points 1
Carbohydrate Points ½
Cholesterol Points 4

P
F/G
C

A
C
CALCIUM
CALCIO

1	pound (460 g) sausage or ground turkey, browned
2	teaspoons sage (add only when using turkey)
6	slices white bread, cubed and crust removed
2	cups (480 ml) skim milk
4	eggs, beaten
1	teaspoon prepared mustard
½	teaspoon salt
¼	pound (120 g) cheddar cheese, grated
	parsley, minced (optional)

Egg Casserole

Serves: 12
Preparation Time: 1 hour, 15 minutes
(refrigerate overnight)

Mix all of the above ingredients together. Lightly coat 13" (33 cm) chef pan with cooking oil spray. Pour mixed ingredients into pan, cover and refrigerate overnight. Bake in 350°F (180°C) oven 1 hour removing lid last 15 minutes or place on top of stove over medium heat 15 minutes, reduce to low 45 minutes leaving covered. Sprinkle top with minced parsley.

NUTRITIONAL BREAKDOWN
PER SERVING
Calories 175
Fat Grams 9
Carbohydrate Grams 9
Protein Grams 13
Cholesterol mg 159
Sodium mg 427
THE POINT SYSTEM
Calorie Points 2½
Protein Points 2
Fat Grams 9
Sodium Points 18½
Fiber Points 0
Carbohydrate Points ½
Chosesterol Points 16

F/G P
C

CALCIUM
CALCIO

Breakfast Burritos

2   pounds (1 kg) mild Italian sausage
2-3   tablespoons chili powder
1   teaspoon cumin
1   tablespoon paprika
¼   cup (60 ml) skim milk
12   eggs or equivalent egg substitutes*
2   tablespoons low calorie margarine
24   8" (20 cm) flour tortillas**
       salsa (recipe below)

Brown sausage and spices over medium heat in large frypan. Mix milk and eggs together with wire whisk. In another frypan melt butter and scramble eggs. Drain sausage on paper towels, add to scrambled eggs. Place 2 heaping tablespoons egg mixture in individual tortilla shells and "burrito" roll. Add salsa to taste. Serve immediately.

*Nutritional breakdown uses egg substitutes and includes salsa.

**see tortillas, page 89

Yields: 2 dozen ❖ Serves: 12
Preparation Time: 20 minutes

❖   ❖   ❖

Salsa

Yields: 2½ cups
Preparation Time: 10 minutes

4   Roma tomatoes, chopped
¼   cup cilantro, chopped
½   white onion, chopped
½   lemon, juiced
       salt and pepper to taste

Mix together in bowl.

NUTRITIONAL BREAKDOWN
PER SERVING
Calories 134
Fat Grams 18
Carbohydrate Grams 21
Protein Grams 15
Cholesterol mg 0
Sodium mg 299
THE POINT SYSTEM
Calorie Points 2
Protein Points 2
Fat Grams 18
Sodium Points 13
Fiber Points 0
Carbohydrate Points 1½
Cholesterol Points 0

Frozen
Strawberry Jam

Serves: 16
Preparation Time: 20 minutes

1   quart whole strawberries
1   cup (240 ml) cherry juice concentrate
1   packet unflavored gelatin
1   teaspoon lemon juice

Wash strawberries and remove stems. Mash with potato masher. Bring cherry juice to boil in 2-quart saucepan (2 L utensil). Add gelatin and stir 1 minute. Remove from heat; stir in strawberries and lemon juice. For individual serving pour into ice cube trays and when frozen, pop out of trays and place in large plastic bags and return to freezer.

NUTRITIONAL BREAKDOWN
PER SERVING

Calories 19
Fat Grams 0
Carbohydrate Grams 4
Protein Grams 1
Cholesterol mg 0
Sodium mg 1
THE POINT SYSTEM
Calorie Points 0
Protein Points 0
Fat Grams 0
Sodium Points 0
Fiber Points 0

F/G P

C

C

Egg Fu Yung

Serves: 4
Preparation Time: 30 minutes

❖   ❖   ❖

5	eggs or equivalent egg substitutes*
½	cup shredded cooked meat, poultry or fish
1	celery rib, finely chopped
4	Chinese dried mushrooms, soaked in boiling water 5 minutes
2	ounces (60 g) bean sprouts
1	small onion, thinly sliced
1	pinch salt
1	pinch pepper
1	tablespoon oil or vegetable cooking spray

SAUCE

1	tablespoon cornstarch
3	tablespoons water
1	cup (240 ml) chicken broth
1	teaspoon ketchup
1	pinch salt
1	pinch pepper
1	dash sesame oil
1	tablespoon soy sauce

In medium bowl beat the eggs slightly, add shredded meat and celery. Squeeze all the liquid from the mushrooms, remove stems, cut caps into thin slices, add to egg mixture. Add bean sprouts and onions to egg mixture and salt and pepper. Spray large frypan with cooking spray or use 1 tablespoon vegetable oil. Place over medium heat. When hot, spoon in about 1/3 cup of egg mixture. Brown one side, turn gently, brown second side. Remove to platter and continue with remaining egg mixture. Combine all of the sauce ingredients in 1-quart saucepan (1.5 L utensil) bring to boil, stirring until thickened. Pour sauce over Egg Fu Yung and serve.

*Nutritional breakdown uses egg substitutes.

Note: To reduce sodium mg by 325 per serving omit soy sauce.

NUTRITIONAL BREAKDOWN
PER SERVING
Calories 138
Fat Grams 5
Carbohydrate Grams 10
Protein Grams 13
Cholesterol mg 13
Sodium mg 1100
THE POINT SYSTEM
Calorie Points 1½
Protein Points 1½
Fat Grams 5
Sodium Points 47
Fiber Points 0
Carbohydrate Points 1/2
Cholesterol Points 1

2 cups (480 ml) dry white wine
1 tablespoon lemon juice
1 pound (460 g) Gruyere, shredded
1 pound (460 g) Fontina, shredded
1 tablespoon arrowroot
2 ounces (60 ml) kirsch (optional)
1 pinch nutmeg
1 loaf French bread, cubed
4 pears, cut in wedges
4 apples, cut in wedges

Cheese Fondue

Serves: 12
Preparation Time: 20 minutes

In 2-quart saucepan (2 L utensil) over medium heat, warm wine and lemon juice to boiling. Reduce to low. Toss cheeses with arrowroot and gradually add cheese mixture to wine, stirring constantly. When cheeses are melted stir in kirsch. Sprinkle top with nutmeg and serve with French bread, apples and pears.

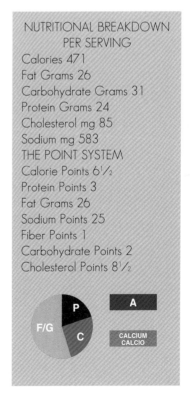

NUTRITIONAL BREAKDOWN
PER SERVING
Calories 471
Fat Grams 26
Carbohydrate Grams 31
Protein Grams 24
Cholesterol mg 85
Sodium mg 583
THE POINT SYSTEM
Calorie Points 6½
Protein Points 3
Fat Grams 26
Sodium Points 25
Fiber Points 1
Carbohydrate Points 2
Cholesterol Points 8½

Vegetables

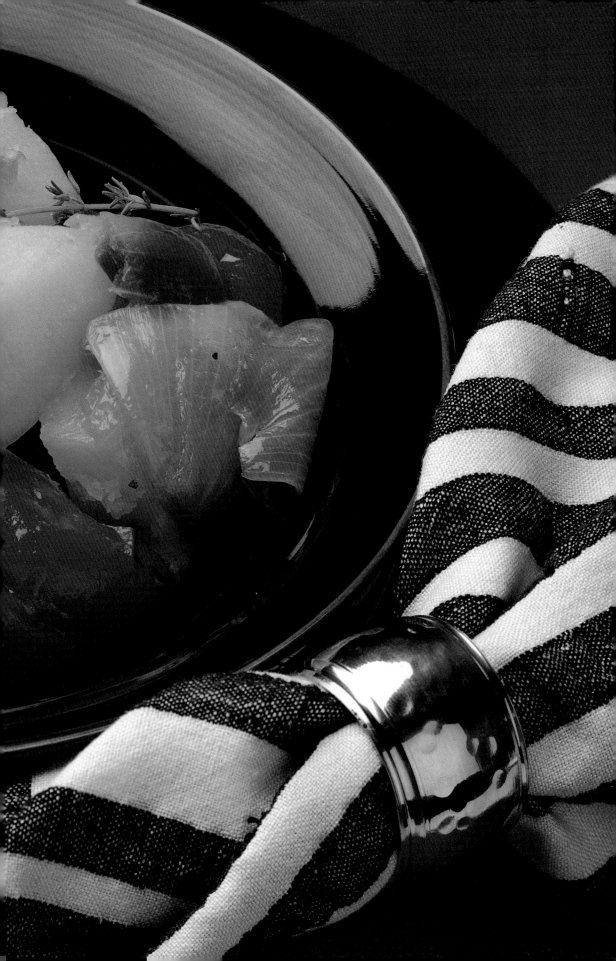

Potato Salad

Serves: 20
Preparation Time: 1 hour

10	medium red potatoes, cooked, peeled and cubed
½	cup celery, chopped
½	cup red onion, chopped
1	cup sour cream or low-fat plain yogurt
½	cup diet mayonnaise
½	teaspoon onion powder
½	teaspoon garlic powder
½	teaspoon pepper
½	teaspoon celery salt
2	eggs, hard cooked,* quartered
1	tomato, quartered
¼	cup green onion, chopped

In large bowl combine potatoes with next eight ingredients. Toss well. Top potato salad with eggs, tomato, and green onion. Refrigerate until ready to serve.

*See instructions on hard cooked eggs on page 19.

NUTRITIONAL BREAKDOWN
PER SERVING
Calories 32
Fat Grams 0
Carbohydrate Grams 7
Protein Grams 1
Cholesterol mg 0
Sodium mg 124
THE POINT SYSTEM
Calorie Points ½
Protein Points 0
Fat Grams 0
Sodium Points 5
Fiber Points 0
Carbohydrate Points ½
Cholesterol Points 0

2	teaspoons safflower oil
1	tablespoon garlic, minced
1	tablespoon ginger
½	teaspoon crushed red pepper
1½	pounds (700 g) carrots, scraped and cut in diagonal pieces
⅔	cup (160 ml) canned chicken broth, undiluted
3	tablespoons soy sauce
2	tablespoons cider vinegar
2	teaspoons sugar
1	tablespoon cornstarch
2	tablespoons water

Spicy Carrots

Serves: 6
Preparation Time: 20 minutes

In 10" chef pan or large frypan heat oil. Place over medium-high heat until hot. Add garlic, ginger, and red pepper, stirring well. Add carrots, chicken broth, soy sauce, cider vinegar, and sugar; stir. Bring to a boil; cover, reduce heat, and simmer 10 minutes or until carrots are crisp-tender.

Combine cornstarch and water, stirring until smooth. Stir cornstarch mixture into carrot mixture and cook 1 minute or until slightly thickened.

NUTRITIONAL BREAKDOWN
PER SERVING
Calories 84
Fat Grams 2
Carbohydrate Grams 16
Protein Grams 2
Cholesterol mg 0
Sodium mg 641
THE POINT SYSTEM
Calorie Points 1
Protein Points 0
Fat Grams 2
Sodium Points 28
Fiber Points 1
Carbohydrate Points 1
Cholesterol Points 0

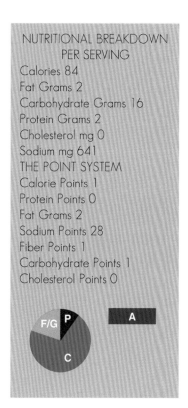

Vegetable Stir Fry

Serves: 4
Preparation Time: 25 minutes

2	teaspoons oil
1	cup broccoli florets, cut into 1" (2.5 cm) pieces
⅔	cup carrots, sliced to 1/8" (0.5 cm)
⅔	cup zucchini, 1/2" (1.5 cm) cubes
1	red onion, sliced
1	tablespoon water
½	cup fresh mushrooms, sliced
¼	teaspoon dill weed
¼	teaspoon salt
4	cherry tomatoes, halved

Heat oil in wok or large frypan over medium-high heat. Add broccoli, carrots, zucchini and onion. Stir-fry over moderate heat about 4 minutes, turning vegetable pieces constantly.

Add water, cover and cook until vegetables are tender-crisp, about 6 minutes.

Stir in mushrooms, dill weed, and salt.

Place tomato halves in vegetable mixture. Cover and cook just until mushrooms and tomatoes are heated, about 3 minutes.

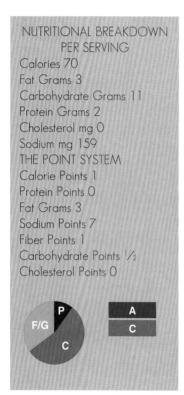

NUTRITIONAL BREAKDOWN
PER SERVING
Calories 70
Fat Grams 3
Carbohydrate Grams 11
Protein Grams 2
Cholesterol mg 0
Sodium mg 159
THE POINT SYSTEM
Calorie Points 1
Protein Points 0
Fat Grams 3
Sodium Points 7
Fiber Points 1
Carbohydrate Points ½
Cholesterol Points 0

2	tablespoons chicken broth
¼	pound (120 g) fresh mushrooms, sliced
¼	cup red pepper, diced
2	tablespoons onion, chopped
1	16 ounce (460 g) can asparagus cuts and tips, drained or 1 pound fresh asparagus
¼	cup (60 ml) dry white wine
1	teaspoon cornstarch
1	teaspoon fresh tarragon leaves, chopped
1	teaspoon lemon peel, grated
1	teaspoon lemon juice
¼	teaspoon salt (optional)
	ground black pepper

Asparagus Mushroom Sauté

Serves: 4
Preparation Time: 15 minutes

Heat chicken broth in 10" chef pan or large frypan over medium-high heat. Add mushrooms, red pepper and onion; sauté about 2 minutes or until almost tender. Add asparagus and sauté about 1 minute. Combine wine and cornstarch; stir to dissolve. Add remaining ingredients to asparagus mixture; stir-fry about 1 minute or until sauce boils and thickens.

NUTRITIONAL BREAKDOWN
PER SERVING
Calories 57
Fat Grams 1
Carbohydrate Grams 6
Protein Grams 4
Cholesterol mg 0
Sodium mg 42
THE POINT SYSTEM
Calorie Points 1/2
Protein Points 1/2
Fat Grams 1
Sodium Points 2
Fiber Points 1
Carbohydrate Points 1/2
Cholesterol Points 0

Eggplant Parmigiana

Serves: 8
Preparation Time: 1 hour

3	medium eggplants
½	teaspoon salt
1	tablespoon olive oil
3	cups (720 ml) tomato sauce or Marinara Sauce*
2	cups mushrooms, sliced
3	cups mozzarella cheese, shredded
¼	cup Romano cheese, grated

*Marinara Sauce recipe on facing page.

Slice eggplants in ½" (1.5 cm) thick rings, sprinkle with salt and set aside for 20 minutes. Rinse eggplant and pat dry. In large frypan, fry eggplant in olive oil until golden brown then drain.

In 6-quart (6 L) roaster spread sauce to cover bottom of pan. Place one layer of eggplant in roaster, one layer mushrooms, one layer of mozzarella cheese, a layer of sauce then repeat. Sprinkle with Romano cheese.

Cover, cook over medium heat for 30 minutes.

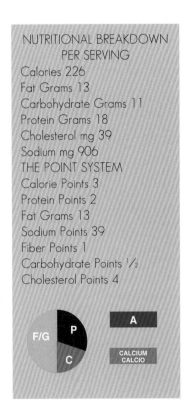

NUTRITIONAL BREAKDOWN
PER SERVING
Calories 226
Fat Grams 13
Carbohydrate Grams 11
Protein Grams 18
Cholesterol mg 39
Sodium mg 906
THE POINT SYSTEM
Calorie Points 3
Protein Points 2
Fat Grams 13
Sodium Points 39
Fiber Points 1
Carbohydrate Points ½
Cholesterol Points 4

Marinara Sauce

pictured with
Eggplant Parmigiana above and
Spinach Cheese Jumbo Shells page 135.

Serves: 12-1 cup servings
Yields: 2 quarts (2 L)
Preparation Time: 1 hour

2	tablespoons olive oil
½	cup onion, chopped
5	cups (1.25 L) water
1	12 ounce (345 g) can tomato paste
2	tablespoons fresh or dried basil
1	tablespoon oregano
2	tablespoons parsley
½	cup (120 ml) red wine (optional)
1	14.5 ounce (435 g) can diced tomatoes

In 3-quart saucepan (3 L utensil) sauté onion in olive oil over medium heat just until tender. Add water, tomato paste, spices, and wine. Mix well, simmer uncovered 30-45 minutes to reduce. Add diced tomatoes, simmer an additional 15 minutes.

NUTRITIONAL BREAKDOWN PER SERVING

Calories 73
Fat Grams 3
Carbohydrate Grams 9
Protein Grams 1
Cholesterol mg 0
Sodium mg 330

THE POINT SYSTEM

Calorie Points 1
Protein Points 0
Fat Grams 3
Sodium Points 14
Fiber Points 0
Carbohydrate Points ½
Cholesterol Points 0

Rosemary Potatoes

Serves: 8
Preparation Time: 1 hour 10 minutes

1	tablespoon olive oil
1	tablespoon butter
1	tablespoon rosemary
1	teaspoon thyme
½	red pepper, cubed
½	onion, quartered
4	¾ pound (345 g) baking potatoes, peeled and cut into 1½" (4 cm) chunks

In 4-quart (4 L) utensil, melt butter in olive oil. Add all other ingredients and toss to coat. Cover and cook over low heat 1 hour, turning after first 30 minutes.

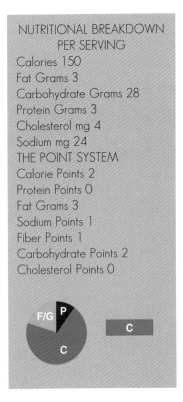

NUTRITIONAL BREAKDOWN
PER SERVING
Calories 150
Fat Grams 3
Carbohydrate Grams 28
Protein Grams 3
Cholesterol mg 4
Sodium mg 24
THE POINT SYSTEM
Calorie Points 2
Protein Points 0
Fat Grams 3
Sodium Points 1
Fiber Points 1
Carbohydrate Points 2
Cholesterol Points 0

3	tablespoons curry spice mix*
3	tablespoons vinegar
¼	cup (60 ml) peanut oil
2	onions, chopped
2	cloves garlic, minced
4	¾ pound (345 g) potatoes, cut into 2 inch cubes
1	pound (460 g) mushrooms, quartered
½	teaspoon salt
1	16 ounce (460 g) can diced tomatoes
1	cup (240 ml) unsweetened coconut milk
½	teaspoon garam masala*
1	8 ounce (230 g) package frozen peas

Vegetable Curry

Serves: 8
Preparation Time: 40 minutes

Mix curry spice with vinegar to form paste, set aside. Heat oil in 6-quart (6 L) roaster over medium heat. Add onions and garlic; sauté until deep gold. Add curry spice paste and fry for 3 minutes stirring constantly. Add potatoes, mushrooms and salt, mix well. Cover and reduce to low for 20 minutes. Add tomatoes, cover and simmer additional 5 minutes. Add coconut milk, garam masala, and peas. Stir and simmer uncovered until heated through.

*See recipes for Curry Spice Mix and Garam Masala in the Spice section, page 201.

Serve with Raita, page 58 and Chicken Satay, page 106.

NUTRITIONAL BREAKDOWN
PER SERVING
Calories 264
Fat Grams 15
Carbohydrate Grams 30
Protein Grams 6
Cholesterol mg 0
Sodium mg 268
THE POINT SYSTEM
Calorie Points 3½
Protein Points 1
Fat Grams 15
Sodium Points 12
Fiber Points 2
Carbohydrate Points 2
Cholesterol Points 0

P
F/G   C

A
C

IRON
HIERRO

Vegetarian Spring Rolls

Serves: 8
Preparation Time: 40 minutes

2	ounces (60 g) bean threads
1	cup carrots, grated
1	red onion, grated
1	red pepper, grated
1	small head green cabbage, grated
1½	tablespoons garlic, minced
1	tablespoon soy sauce
1	teaspoon ginger, grated
2	eggs
1	package spring roll wrappers

Soak bean threads in warm water for 10 minutes. Drain and set aside.

Using food cutter cone #2 or hand grater, grate carrots, red onion, red pepper, cabbage, and garlic into large bowl. Add soy sauce, ginger, and eggs to bowl and mix well. In separate bowl, mix together ½ cup (120 ml) water and 1 tablespoon cornstarch to seal edges. "Burrito" roll each wrapper by placing approximately 2 tablespoons filling one-third the way up the spring roll wrapper. Fold corner over filling forming lightly packed log shaped roll. Fold side edges over and roll to end of wrapper. Seal edges with cornstarch and water mixture and finish rolling. Repeat with other wrappers.

Note: Keep wrappers moist prior to rolling, a damp paper towel over wrappers before use keeps moisture in. If they should dry, lightly dampen with sprinkle of water prior to filling each wrapper.

Spring rolls may be deep fried or steamed.

TO FRY
Heat 2" (5 cm) of oil to 375°F (190°C) in wok or large fry pan. Fry 2 or 3 rolls at a time until they are firm and golden brown, approximately 4 minutes.
Serve with Soy Dipping Sauce shown on next page.

TO STEAM
Bring 2" (5 cm) of water to boil in bottom of 6-quart (6 L) roaster. Spray steamer rack with cooking spray. Place wrapped spring rolls on steamer rack, cover and steam to heat through. To keep warm leave covered and turn off heat. They will stay warm for 1 hour.

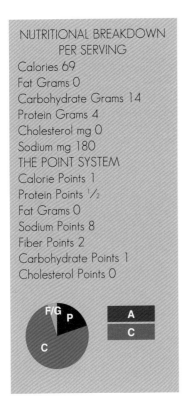

NUTRITIONAL BREAKDOWN
PER SERVING
Calories 69
Fat Grams 0
Carbohydrate Grams 14
Protein Grams 4
Cholesterol mg 0
Sodium mg 180
THE POINT SYSTEM
Calorie Points 1
Protein Points ½
Fat Grams 0
Sodium Points 8
Fiber Points 2
Carbohydrate Points 1
Cholesterol Points 0

Soy Dipping Sauce

Yields: 2 cups (480 ml)
Preparation Time: 10 minutes

½   cup (120 ml) water
½   cup (120 ml) white vinegar
½   cup (120 ml) soy sauce
½   cup sugar
1   teaspoon ground chili paste
2   teaspoons garlic, chopped

Mix all ingredients in small bowl.

NUTRITIONAL BREAKDOWN
PER SERVING
Calories 71
Fat Grams 0
Carbohydrate Grams 17
Protein Grams 2
Cholesterol mg 0
Sodium mg 538
THE POINT SYSTEM
Calorie Points 1
Protein Points 1
Fat Grams 0
Sodium Points 23
Fiber Points 0
Carbohydrate Points 1
Cholesterol Points 0

Stuffed Artichokes

Serves: 4
Preparation Time: 45 minutes to 1 hour

4	artichokes
	juice of 1 lemon
1¼	cups fine bread crumbs
1	clove garlic, minced
¼	cup parsley, chopped
¼	cup Parmesan cheese, grated
¼	teaspoon dried basil
⅛	teaspoon dried crushed red pepper
2	tablespoons olive oil
2	tablespoons dry white wine

Wash and trim stems and remove loose outer leaves from artichokes. Cut off ½" (1.5 cm) of tops. Snip off leaf tips with kitchen shears. Brush edges with lemon juice.

Combine remaining ingredients. Starting at bottom and working up stuff a small amount of mixture on each leaf of artichoke.

Bring 2 cups (480 ml) of water to boil in 6-quart (6 L) roaster. Place artichokes in steamer of roaster, cover, reduce heat to medium-low. Steam artichokes, over boiling water 30 minutes or until leaf easily pulls off.

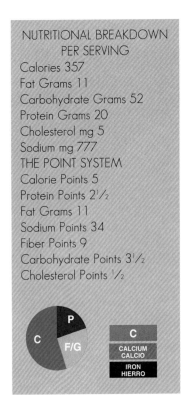

NUTRITIONAL BREAKDOWN
PER SERVING
Calories 357
Fat Grams 11
Carbohydrate Grams 52
Protein Grams 20
Cholesterol mg 5
Sodium mg 777
THE POINT SYSTEM
Calorie Points 5
Protein Points 2½
Fat Grams 11
Sodium Points 34
Fiber Points 9
Carbohydrate Points 3½
Cholesterol Points ½

2	slices bacon, chopped (optional)
4	cups red cabbage, shredded
1	green pepper, shredded
2	cups celery, diced
2	medium onions, sliced
2	tomatoes, chopped
2	teaspoons sugar
	salt and pepper to taste

In large frypan brown bacon over medium heat, remove bacon, reduce heat to medium-low. Add cabbage, green pepper, celery and onion. Cover and cook 15 minutes, stir and add tomatoes. Cover and cook an additional 10-15 minutes. Sprinkle with sugar, salt and pepper to taste. Stir and enjoy.

Skillet Cabbage

Serves: 8
Preparation Time: 30 minutes

NUTRITIONAL BREAKDOWN
PER SERVING
Calories 64
Fat Grams 1
Carbohydrate Grams 13
Protein Grams 2
Cholesterol mg 1
Sodium mg 60
THE POINT SYSTEM
Calorie Points 1
Protein Points 0
Fat Grams 1
Sodium Points 3
Fiber Points 2
Carbohydrate Points 1
Cholesterol Points 0

F/G P
C
C

Italian Focaccia

Focaccia is as flavorful as a simple country bread can get. Olive oil and fresh rosemary give this yeast-raised flatbread its glorious Italian flavor.

Serves: 8
Preparation Time: 1 hour, 50 minutes
(1 hour, 30 minutes rising time)

1	package active dry yeast
1	cup (240 ml) warm water (105°-115°F/41°-46°C)
2½	tablespoons fresh rosemary, snipped
3	tablespoons olive oil
2	teaspoons salt
2½-3	cups all purpose flour
	coarsely ground black pepper (optional)

Dissolve yeast in warm water in large bowl. Stir in rosemary, oil, salt and enough flour to make dough easy to handle. Turn dough onto lightly floured surface; knead until smooth and elastic, 5-10 minutes. Place in greased bowl; turn greased side up. Cover; let rise in warm place until it doubles, about 1 hour. (Dough is ready if indentation remains when touched.)

Punch down dough. Press into oiled 13" (33 cm) chef pan. Make depressions, with fingers about 2" (5 cm) apart, on top of dough. Brush with oil and sprinkle with pepper. Let rise uncovered 30 minutes. Cook covered on medium heat for 15 minutes. Reduce heat to low and continue to cook with the vents open for 10 more minutes. Bake until golden brown, check when done by gently lifting the bottom with a spatula. Brush with additional oil. Serve warm.

Note: For a darker crust on the top; after the first 15 minutes of cooking time on the stove, the chef pan can be placed in the oven without the cover and finished cooking at 375°F (190°C) for 10 minutes.

NUTRITIONAL BREAKDOWN PER SERVING
Calories 288
Fat Grams 6
Carbohydrate Grams 46
Protein Grams 13
Cholesterol mg 0
Sodium mg 547

THE POINT SYSTEM
Calorie Points 4
Protein Points
Fat Grams 6
Sodium Points 24
Fiber Points 3
Carbohydrate Points 3
Cholesterol Points 0

F/G P
C

IRON
HIERRO

⅓   cup butter
4   eggs
1   cup (240 ml) skim milk
1   cup flour

Dutch Babies
German Pancakes

Place butter in 13" (33 cm) chef pan and place in a 400°F (210°C) oven. While butter melts, mix batter. Put eggs in a blender or food processor and blend at high speed for 1 minute. With motor running, gradually pour in milk, then add flour; continue blending for 30 seconds. Or in a bowl, beat eggs until blended; gradually beat in milk, then flour.

Remove pan from oven and pour in batter. Return pan to oven and bake until pancake is puffy and well browned (20 to 25 minutes).

Dust pancake with ground nutmeg, if you wish. Cut in wedges and serve at once with any of the toppings listed below.

POWDERED SUGAR CLASSIC
Have a shaker or bowl of powdered sugar and thick wedges of lemon at the table. Sprinkle sugar on hot pancake, then squeeze on lemon juice.

FRUIT
Sliced strawberries or peaches, sweetened to taste, or any fruit in season, cut and sweetened.

SYRUP
Pass warm or cold honey, maple syrup, or any favorite fruit syrup or sauce.

Serves: 6
Preparation Time: 35 minutes

❖   ❖   ❖

NUTRITIONAL BREAKDOWN
PER SERVING
(toppings not included)
Calories 192
Fat Grams 10
Carbohydrate Grams 18
Protein Grams 6
Cholesterol mg 28
Sodium mg 162
THE POINT SYSTEM
Calorie Points 2½
Protein Points 1
Fat Grams 10
Sodium Points 7
Fiber Points 0
Carbohydrate Points 1
Cholesterol Points 3

Cornbread

Serves: 16
(or divide in half for small electric pan)
Preparation Time: 65 minutes

4 cups white self-rising cornmeal
3 cups (720 ml) 1% milk
2 eggs
4 tablespoons sugar
2 tablespoons diet margarine

Combine first 4 ingredients and mix thoroughly. Melt margarine in 13" (33 cm) electric pan or chef pan then pour in batter. Lower heat to simmer, cover and cook for one hour.

(A tip when baking on top of the stove or in an electric pan: when removing lid, invert immediately and move from over the top of what is baking. The moisture condenses on the lid and will drip when seal is broken.)

NUTRITIONAL BREAKDOWN
PER SERVING
Calories 162
Fat Grams 2
Carbohydrate Grams 31
Protein Grams 5
Cholesterol mg 2
Sodium mg 511
THE POINT SYSTEM
Calorie Points 2
Protein Points 1
Fat Grams 2
Sodium Points 22
Fiber Points 1
Carbohydrate Points 2
Cholesterol Points 0

F/G P

C

CALCIUM
CALCIO

1	cup quick rolled oats
1	cup all-purpose flour
½	teaspoon salt
2	teaspoons baking powder
1	teaspoon baking soda
¼	cup cold butter
⅔	cup (160 ml) buttermilk

Griddle Oat Scones

Serves: 8
Preparation Time: 20 minutes

Mix the oats, flour, salt, baking powder and baking soda together in a bowl. Using a pastry blender or fork, cut the butter in with the flour mixture until it looks like coarse crumbs. Stir in the buttermilk until the dough holds together. On a floured surface knead the dough, then form into a ball. Flatten it into a circle that is ½" (1.5 cm) thick. Cut into 8 pie-shaped wedges.

Rub a small amount of flour on a cold, large frypan. Heat the pan on medium-low for 5 minutes. Place 3-4 scone wedges in the pan and cook 6-8 minutes on each side. Turn only once. Repeat the process with the uncooked wedges. Serve hot with jam or fruit preserves.

NUTRITIONAL BREAKDOWN
PER SERVING
Calories 156
Fat Grams 7
Carbohydrate Grams 20
Protein Grams 4
Cholesterol mg 16
Sodium mg 444
THE POINT SYSTEM
Calorie Points 2
Protein Points ½
Fat Grams 7
Sodium Points 19
Fiber Points 1
Carbohydrate Points 1½
Cholesterol Points 2

Nan Bread

Baked Leavened Bread
from India

Serves: 4
Preparation Time: 45 minutes

1	cup whole meal wheat flour
1	teaspoon sugar
½	teaspoon baking powder
½	teaspoon salt
3	tablespoons milk
¼	cup plain yogurt
1	ounce (30 g) yeast dissolved in a little of the milk
2	tablespoons butter, melted
1	egg
2	tablespoons butter, melted
	or 1 egg yolk
1	tablespoon poppy seeds

Sift the flour, sugar, baking powder and salt. Warm the milk and yogurt, and add the yeast, butter and egg. Mix to combine thoroughly. Make a depression in the center of the flour and pour in the milk mixture a little at a time until all is absorbed. On floured surface knead well for 15 minutes until smooth and springy, adding a little more flour if the dough is sticky. Cover and leave to rise until double in bulk (approximately 2 hours, unless the weather is hot, in which case the dough might rise in half the time).

Divide into 8 portions and roll into balls with well-floured hands. Cover and set aside for another 15 minutes. Flatten each ball into a thick pancake with the help of a little flour by tossing from one palm of the hand to the other. Brush tops with melted butter or egg yolk and sprinkle with poppy seeds. Cook in a preheated 10" chef pan or large fry-pan on medium heat; when first side is browned, flip and cook other side.

NUTRITIONAL BREAKDOWN
PER SERVING
Calories 343
Fat Grams 10
Carbohydrate Grams 51
Protein Grams 16
Cholesterol mg 69
Sodium mg 435
THE POINT SYSTEM
Calorie Points 4½
Protein Points 2
Fat Grams 10
Sodium Points 19
Fiber Points 3
Carbohydrate Points 3½
Cholesterol Points 7

P
C
F/G

CALCIUM
CALCIO

IRON
HIERRO

1	cup basmati rice
2	cups (480 ml) water
½	teaspoon salt
2	tablespoons olive oil
3	tablespoons butter
1	small onion sliced
2	teaspoons garam masala*
2	cups (480 ml) water
½	cup golden raisins
½	cup frozen peas
¼	cup blanched almonds*

* See recipes for Garam Masala and Blanched Almonds in the Spice section, page 201.

Rinse basmati rice and then soak 1 hour in 2 cups water mixed with salt. Drain rice, which is now very brittle. Be careful not to break. While rice is soaking, heat oil and butter in 6-quart (6 L) roaster over medium heat. Brown onions in oil until light golden brown. (Meanwhile boil garam masala [blend of spices] in 2 cups water.)

Add raisins to onions and cook additional 5 minutes. Remove raisins and a few onions - save for garnish. Pour boiling water mixture and spices into onions, then add rice gently; do not break, do not stir. Cover and bring to boil 7-10 minutes, then reduce to low. Sprinkle in frozen peas. Cover and cook an additional 5 minutes.

To serve, lift out of pan with large spoon to serving dish, garnish with reserved onions and raisins and blanched almonds.

Basmati Pea Pilaf
Matar Polao

Serves: 6
Preparation Time: 1 hour, 15 minutes

NUTRITIONAL BREAKDOWN
PER SERVING
Calories 350
Fat Grams 18
Carbohydrate Grams 42
Protein Grams 9
Cholesterol mg 10
Sodium mg 233
THE POINT SYSTEM
Calorie Points 4½
Protein Points 1
Fat Grams 18
Sodium Points 10
Fiber Points 2
Carbohydrate Points 3
Cholesterol Points 1

Hom Bow

Yields: 10 buns
Preparation Time: 15 minutes
(1 hour rising time)
Cooking Time: 15 to 25 minutes

1¼ cups (300 ml) skim milk
1   tablespoon active dry yeast
1   tablespoon sugar
1   tablespoon vegetable oil
½   teaspoon salt
3½   cups (approximately) flour, all-purpose

FILLING
2   tablespoons onion, finely chopped
1   clove garlic, minced
1   tablespoon cooking oil (peanut oil)
½   pound (230 g) ground pork
⅓   cup (80 ml) water
2   tablespoons soy sauce
2   teaspoons cornstarch
2   teaspoons sugar
½   teaspoon ginger

In a 2-quart saucepan (2 L utensil) heat milk just till warm. Stir together warm milk, yeast, sugar, oil, and salt. Add ½ of the flour and blend together thoroughly. Stir in enough remaining flour to make a soft dough that can be kneaded. Knead lightly on floured board. Return to a lightly greased bowl, turning once to grease surface. Cover and let rise in a warm place until double (approximately 45-60 minutes).

During the rising time, make the filling by cooking in the 2-quart saucepan (2 L utensil) over medium heat, onion and garlic in the oil until the onion is tender but not brown. Add the pork and cook until browned. Stir water and soy sauce into cornstarch; add the 2 teaspoons sugar and ginger. Add to pork mixture. Cook and stir until thickened; remove from heat. Keep in the refrigerator until ready to use.

When the rising period is finished; punch the dough down, turn out onto a lightly floured surface. Shape into 10 balls (or more depending on size preference). Cover, let rest 5 minutes.

On a lightly floured surface, flatten each ball of dough to a 3½" (9 cm) circle. Place a rounded spoonful of pork mixture in center of each dough circle. Bring edges of dough up around filling, stretching a little until edges just meet; pinch to seal.

THESE PORK-FILLED BUNS CAN BE STEAMED OR BAKED.

TO STEAM
Place 1 cup (240 ml) of water in the bottom of the large frypan. Bring the water to steaming. Add the steamer tray which has been greased, and place the buns on the steamer tray. Cover, and steam on medium heat for 15 minutes.

TO BAKE
Place 5 buns in a greased chef pan. Bake in a 375°F (190°C) oven for 25 minutes, or until golden brown.

NUTRITIONAL BREAKDOWN
PER SERVING
Calories 265
Fat Grams 8
Carbohydrate Grams 39
Protein Grams 10
Cholesterol mg 14
Sodium mg 484
THE POINT SYSTEM
Calorie Points 3½
Protein Points 1
Fat Grams 8
Fiber Points 0
Carbohydrate Points 2½
Cholesterol Points 1

F/G P

C

Spicy Wehani with Cashews

Serves: 4 ❖ Yields: 4 cups (1 L)
Preparation Time: 1 hour, 10 minutes

3	tablespoons chicken broth
2	teaspoons cumin seed
¼	teaspoon ground cloves
1	bay leaf
¼	teaspoon red hot pepper flakes
1	onion, minced
2	cloves garlic, minced
1	cup Wehani rice, uncooked
2¼	cups (540 ml) hot water
½	teaspoon salt
¼	cup roasted cashews, chopped

Heat chicken broth in large saucepan over medium heat. Add cumin seeds, cloves and bay leaf; stir until fragrant about 15 seconds. Add red pepper, onion and garlic: sauté until onion is softened. Stir in rice and coat; cook about two minutes. Add water and salt; stir, cover and reduce heat to low. Do not remove lid for 40 minutes. Remove from heat, keep covered additional 15 minutes. Remove bay leaf. Stir in cashews just prior to serving.

NUTRITIONAL BREAKDOWN
PER SERVING
Calories 130
Fat Grams 5
Carbohydrate Grams 19
Protein Grams 4
Cholesterol mg 0
Sodium mg 311
THE POINT SYSTEM
Calorie Points 1½
Protein Points 0
Fat Grams 5
Sodium Points 14
Fiber Points 1
Carbohydrate Points 1
Cholesterol Points 0

2	tablespoons olive oil
1	teaspoon ground cinnamon
1	teaspoon cumin
1	teaspoon paprika
4	chicken thighs, skinned
1	onion, sliced thin
1	cup parsnips, diced
¾	cup carrots, sliced
½	cup celery, chopped
10	dried apricot halves
1	15 ounce (430 g) can diced tomatoes
3	cups (720 ml) water
1¼	cups couscous
2	tablespoons cilantro, chopped
	salt and pepper to taste

Couscous with Chicken Thighs

Serves: 4
Preparation Time: 50 minutes

❖   ❖   ❖

Heat olive oil in large frypan over medium heat. Add cinnamon, cumin and paprika stirring until fragrant. Add chicken thighs, turn to low heat and cover. After 5 minutes turn chicken and add onion, parsnips, carrots, celery and apricots. Cover and cook 5 minutes. Add tomatoes and water. Cover and simmer 30 minutes. Remove from heat, place chicken on platter and keep warm. Add couscous, cover, let stand 5 minutes. To serve mound couscous on platter around thighs. Sprinkle cilantro on top.

NUTRITIONAL BREAKDOWN
PER SERVING
Calories 415
Fat Grams 14
Carbohydrate Grams 56
Protein Grams 20
Cholesterol mg 49
Sodium mg 295
THE POINT SYSTEM
Calorie Points 5 1/2
Protein Points 3
Fat Grams 14
Sodium Points 13
Fiber Points 5
Carbohydrate Points 4
Cholesterol Points 5

Chinese "Not Fried" Rice

Serves: 6
Preparation Time: 35 minutes

½	cup onion, finely chopped
2	cups (480 ml) chicken broth, undiluted
1	tablespoon dry sherry
1	tablespoon soy sauce
1	teaspoon dark sesame oil
1	cup uncooked long grain converted rice
⅓	cup green onions, diagonally sliced
1	tablespoon pine nuts, toasted

In 2-quart saucepan (2 L utensil) over medium heat, sauté onions, covered for 2 minutes or until tender. Add chicken broth, sherry, soy sauce, and sesame oil; bring to a boil. Stir in rice; cover, reduce heat, and simmer 25 minutes or until rice is tender and liquid is absorbed. Remove from heat, and stir in green onions and pine nuts.

NUTRITIONAL BREAKDOWN
PER SERVING
Calories 86
Fat Grams 2
Carbohydrate Grams 11
Protein Grams 3
Cholesterol mg 0
Sodium mg 432
THE POINT SYSTEM
Calorie Points 1
Protein Points 0
Fat Grams 2
Sodium Points 19
Fiber Points 0
Carbohydrate Points ½
Cholesterol Points 0

3	tablespoons oil
½	small onion, chopped
2	cloves garlic, chopped
1½	cups (360 ml) canned Italian plum tomatoes, crushed
4	quarts (4 L) water
½	teaspoon salt
1	pound (460 g) rigatoni, penne or fusilli, cooked
1	tablespoon capers
½	cup black olives, chopped
3	tablespoons fresh basil, chopped
1	teaspoon dried red pepper flakes
½	cup Romano cheese, grated

Pasta Puttánesca

Heat oil in 2-quart saucepan (2 L utensil) over medium heat. Add onion, garlic and sauté until transparent. Reduce heat to low. Add tomatoes, cover, cook for 25 minutes. While sauce is cooking, heat water to boiling in pasta pan or 6-quart (6 L) utensil with pasta insert; when boiling add salt and pasta. Cook pasta until al dente (firm to the bite). Remove insert to drain. Pour into pasta bowl. Add capers, olives, basil and red pepper flakes to sauce. Simmer an additional 10 minutes. Pour over cooked pasta. Serve immediately, passing the grated Romano cheese.

Serves: 6
Preparation Time: 30 minutes

❖   ❖   ❖

NUTRITIONAL BREAKDOWN
PER SERVING
Calories 371
Fat Grams 16
Carbohydrate Grams 48
Protein Grams 13
Cholesterol mg 101
Sodium mg 326
THE POINT SYSTEM
Calorie Points 5
Protein Points 2
Fat Grams 16
Sodium Points 14
Fiber Points 1
Carbohydrate Points 3
Cholesterol Points 10

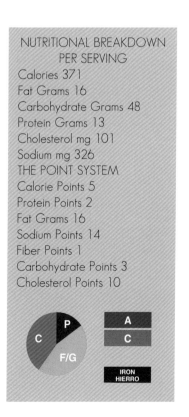

Pasta Carbonara

Serves: 10
Preparation Time: 30 minutes

½	teaspoon salt
1	pound (460 g) penne pasta
½	pound (230 g) pancetta* in ½" (1.5 cm) slices
⅓	cup Romano cheese, grated
⅓	cup Parmesan cheese, grated
4	eggs

Bring 4 quarts of water to boil in pasta pan or 6-quart (6 L) utensil with insert. When boiling add pasta. Stir, cook until al dente (firm to the bite). Remove insert from pan to drain. In 6 quart (6 L) utensil, cook pancetta over medium heat until it clarifies; add cooked pasta and stir well; remove from heat. Slowly add cheeses alternating cheeses and stirring well. Continue stirring pasta to cool it, slowly add eggs stirring quickly to keep eggs from curdling. Garnish with Italian parsley.

*If pancetta (Italian bacon) is not available substitute thick sliced bacon.

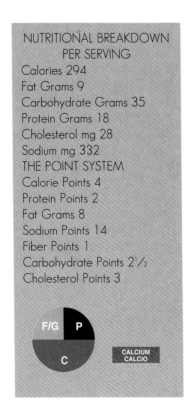

NUTRITIONAL BREAKDOWN
PER SERVING
Calories 294
Fat Grams 9
Carbohydrate Grams 35
Protein Grams 18
Cholesterol mg 28
Sodium mg 332
THE POINT SYSTEM
Calorie Points 4
Protein Points 2
Fat Grams 8
Sodium Points 14
Fiber Points 1
Carbohydrate Points 2½
Cholesterol Points 3

F/G P
C
CALCIUM
CALCIO

Pasta Shrimp Salad

3 celery ribs
3 sweet pickles
3 hard boiled eggs
3 green onions
1½ cups shrimp, boiled and shelled
3 cups cooked pasta
1 cup pineapple tidbits and juice
½ cup fat free mayonnaise
   salt and pepper to taste
   cold shredded lettuce

Serves: 4
Preparation Time: 30 minutes

Coarsely chop celery, pickles, eggs, and onions. Combine all ingredients, except lettuce, toss in a large salad bowl. Add salt and pepper if desired. Serve on cold shredded lettuce.

NUTRITIONAL BREAKDOWN
PER SERVING
Calories 299
Fat Grams 5
Carbohydrate Grams 50
Protein Grams 13
Cholesterol mg 187
Sodium mg 581
THE POINT SYSTEM
Calorie Points 4
Protein Points 2
Fat Grams 5
Sodium Points 25
Fiber Points 1
Carbohydrate Points 3½
Cholesterol Points 19

F/G P
C

Pasta Primavera

Serves: 8 ❖ Yields: 2 quarts (2 L)
Preparation Time: 30 minutes

1	clove garlic, minced
¼	pound (115 g) fresh mushrooms, sliced
½	cup broccoli floretes
½	cup fresh snow pea pods
½	cup yellow squash, sliced
½	cup zucchini, sliced
1	tablespoon fresh chives, chopped
8	ounces (230 g) fresh linguine, uncooked
¼	cup (60 ml) hot water
2	tablespoons Chablis or dry white wine
¼	teaspoon chicken-flavored bouillon
¾	cup (180 ml) skim milk
1	tablespoon all-purpose flour
¼	cup + 1 tablespoon fresh Parmesan cheese, grated, divided
1	tablespoon fresh parsley, chopped
1½	teaspoons basil, chopped
	fresh ground black pepper to taste

In large frypan over medium heat lightly brown garlic and mushrooms. Add remaining vegetables, and cover for 15-20 minutes or until vegetables are crisp-tender. Set aside.

Cook linguine according to package directions, omitting salt and fat. Drain and set aside.

Combine water, wine and bouillon in a 1-quart saucepan (1.5 L utensil) and heat to boiling.

Combine milk and flour in a small bowl; stir well. Gradually add flour mixture to wine mixture, stirring constantly. Cook over medium heat, stirring constantly, 5 minutes or until thickened and bubbly. Pour sauce over linguine, and toss gently. Add ¼ cup Parmesan cheese, parsley, basil, and toss gently. Transfer linguine mixture to a large serving platter, and top with reserved vegetable mixture; sprinkle with remaining 1 tablespoon Parmesan cheese.

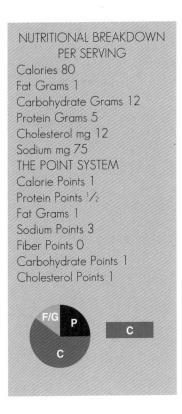

NUTRITIONAL BREAKDOWN
PER SERVING
Calories 80
Fat Grams 1
Carbohydrate Grams 12
Protein Grams 5
Cholesterol mg 12
Sodium mg 75
THE POINT SYSTEM
Calorie Points 1
Protein Points ½
Fat Grams 1
Sodium Points 3
Fiber Points 0
Carbohydrate Points 1
Cholesterol Points 1

Reduced Calorie Fettucini

Serves: 12-1 cup servings
Preparation Time: 20 minutes

1	12 ounce (340 g) package fettucini noodles
½	cup low-fat plain yogurt
½	cup Parmesan cheese, grated
1	tablespoon fresh pepper, coarsely ground
2	tablespoons fresh parsley, chopped
1	teaspoon salt (optional)

Using pasta pan or 6-quart (6 L) utensil with pasta insert, fill with water and bring to boil. Add salt and fettucini noodles. Cook until al dente (firm to the bite). Remove insert to drain noodles. Place drained noodles in large pasta bowl. Add all other ingredients to bowl. Toss noodles to coat evenly. Add coarse ground pepper to taste. Top with parsley, if desired.

NUTRITIONAL BREAKDOWN
PER SERVING
Calories 75
Fat Grams 2
Carbohydrate Grams 11
Protein Grams 4
Cholesterol mg 16
Sodium mg 265
THE POINT SYSTEM
Calorie Points 1
Protein Points ½
Fat Grams 2
Sodium Points 12
Fiber Points 0
Carbohydrate Points ½
Cholesterol Points 1½

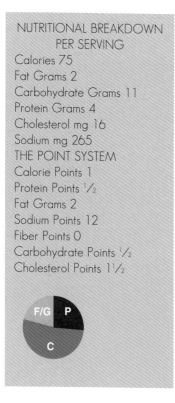

Garlic Bread

Pictured with Basic Lasagna page 85.

Serves: 12
Preparation Time: 10 minutes

4	cloves garlic, minced
¼	cup diet margarine
1	loaf French bread, sliced

Preheat griddle to medium. In 8" chef pan or small frypan sauté fresh garlic in margarine for 1 minute. Dip one side of bread quickly in melted margarine and garlic. Place buttered side down on griddle and grill until brown; approximately 2 minutes.

Soda Bread

Pictured with Blarney Stone Stew page 81.

Yields: 2 dozen
Preparation Time: 1 hour, 10 minutes

4	cups flour
1	teaspoon baking soda
1	teaspoon salt
1	tablespoon butter
½	cup (120 ml) buttermilk

Sift together flour, soda, and salt in large bowl. Cut in butter with fork or pastry cutter. Add buttermilk and stir. Knead dough for several minutes on floured surface. Form dough into 2" (5 cm) balls; slightly flatten. Using a floured knife, cut slits in top of balls. Place balls in large ungreased frypan and cover with 4-quart (4 L) dome cover. Bake over low heat for 45 minutes or until done.

Serve with honey.

NUTRITIONAL BREAKDOWN
PER SERVING
Calories 86
Fat Grams 3
Carbohydrate Grams 13
Protein Grams 2
Cholesterol mg 0
Sodium mg 196
THE POINT SYSTEM
Calorie Points 1
Protein Points 0
Fat Grams 3
Sodium Points 9
Fiber Points 0
Carbohydrate Points 1
Cholesterol Points 0

Calories 246
Fat Grams 2
Carbohydrate Grams 48
Protein Grams 7
Cholesterol mg 4
Sodium mg 456
THE POINT SYSTEM
Calorie Points 3½
Protein Points 1
Fat Grams 2
Sodium Points 19
Fiber Points 1
Carbohydrate Points 3
Cholesterol Points 0

esserts

Chocolate Glazed Poached Pears

Serves: 6
Preparation Time: 45 minutes
(cool before glazing)

6	firm but ripe pears
3	tablespoons (45 ml) water
3	ounces (90 g) German sweet chocolate, chopped
3	ounces (90 g) semisweet chocolate, chopped
¼	cup unsalted butter
	sprigs of mint for garnish (optional)

PEARS

Using a vegetable peeler, peel pears and leave stems intact. If necessary, cut a small slice off each pear's bottom so it will stand upright.
Stand pears in water in the 3-quart saucepan (3 L utensil) and cover. Place pan over low heat for 30 minutes.
As each pear is done. Remove pears with a slotted spoon and place it on a baking sheet or wire rack to cool. Pears may be refrigerated several hours (or overnight), if desired.

GLAZE

Several hours before serving, melt both varieties of chocolate and butter in top of a double boiler over simmering water at low heat, stirring occasionally. When smooth, remove from heat.

Blot all pears dry with paper towels. Line a baking sheet with waxed paper. Holding each pear carefully by its stem, dip each into the chocolate glazing mixture, tilting pear and spooning glaze to cover pear completely. Place on baking sheet and refrigerate for several hours. Before serving, remove each pear with spatula to serving plate, garnish with fresh mint.

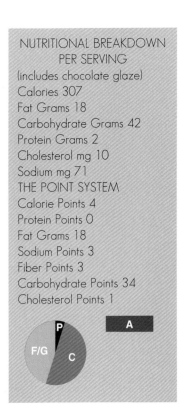

NUTRITIONAL BREAKDOWN
PER SERVING
(includes chocolate glaze)
Calories 307
Fat Grams 18
Carbohydrate Grams 42
Protein Grams 2
Cholesterol mg 10
Sodium mg 71
THE POINT SYSTEM
Calorie Points 4
Protein Points 0
Fat Grams 18
Sodium Points 3
Fiber Points 3
Carbohydrate Points 34
Cholesterol Points 1

P
A
F/G
C

Also shown are fresh, clean strawberries with stems intact, blotted dry, then dipped in glaze mixture.

Fruit and Ginger Pears

Serves: 6
Preparation Time: 50 minutes

6	medium pears
1	8¾ ounce (250 g) can fruit cocktail
⅓	cup (80 ml) orange juice
2	teaspoons crystallized ginger, chopped
1	tablespoon cornstarch
1	tablespoon water
3	tablespoons dry sherry

Core pears. Drain fruit cocktail, reserving syrup. Add water to make ⅔ cup (160 ml) liquid. In deep 4-quart (4 L) utensil combine reserved syrup, orange juice, and ginger. Place whole pears upright in liquid and bring to a boil. Reduce heat; cover and simmer 40 minutes. Remove pears. Combine cornstarch and water; stir into hot liquid in pan. Cook and stir until thickened and bubbly. Remove from heat; stir in sherry and fruit cocktail. Place pears in 6 large wineglasses or sherbets. Spoon fruit cocktail sauce into core cavity and over pears, crowning with cherry half. Serve the sauced pears warm or cool.

NUTRITIONAL BREAKDOWN
PER SERVING
Calories 173
Fat Grams 1
Carbohydrate Grams 41
Protein Grams 1
Cholesterol mg 0
Sodium mg 8
THE POINT SYSTEM
Calorie Points 2½
Protein Points 0
Fat Grams 1
Sodium Points 0
Fiber Points 2
Carbohydrate Points 2½
Cholesterol Points 0

¼	cup + 2 tablespoons diet margarine, softened
⅓	cup cream cheese, softened
⅔	cup sugar
2	eggs, beaten
1	teaspoon vanilla extract
¾	cup all-purpose flour
½	teaspoon baking powder
⅛	teaspoon salt
3	tablespoons unsweetened cocoa

Marbled Brownies

Yields: 2 dozen
Preparation Time: 30 minutes

Cream margarine and cheese; gradually add sugar, beating at medium speed with an electric mixer until light and fluffy. Add eggs and vanilla, beating well. Combine flour, baking powder and salt; add to creamed mixture, beating well. Divide batter in half. Sift cocoa over half of batter and fold in gently. Spoon cocoa mixture into a 10" chef pan or large frypan. Pour remaining half of batter into pan. Gently cut through mixture in pan with a knife to create a marbled effect; cover.

Bake on top of stove at medium-low heat covered for 20 minutes or until a wooden pick inserted in center comes out clean. Cool brownies, then cut into 2" x 1¼" (5 cm x 3.5 cm) bars.

NUTRITIONAL BREAKDOWN
PER SERVING
Calories 57
Fat Grams 2
Carbohydrate Grams 9
Protein Grams 1
Cholesterol mg 2
Sodium mg 74
THE POINT SYSTEM
Calorie Points 1
Protein Points 0
Fat Grams 2
Sodium Points 3
Fiber Points 0
Carbohydrate Points ½
Cholesterol Points 0

Poppy Seed Icebox Cookies

Yields: 64 cookies
Preparation Time: 1 hour

⅓	cup margarine, softened
⅔	cup sugar
1	egg, beaten
2	tablespoons skim milk
½	teaspoon almond extract
1¼	cups all-purpose flour
½	teaspoon baking soda
¼	teaspoon salt
¼	teaspoon ground nutmeg
⅛	cup poppy seeds

Cream margarine; gradually add sugar, beating well at medium speed with electric mixer until light and fluffy. Add egg, beating well. Add skim milk and almond extract. Combine flour, baking soda, salt and nutmeg; add to creamed mixture, beating well. Stir in poppy seeds. Divide dough into 4 equal portions; place each portion on a sheet of plastic wrap, and shape into a 4" x 2" log (10 cm x 5 cm). Wrap logs in plastic wrap, and refrigerate or freeze until firm. Unwrap logs, and cut into ¼" (75 mm) slices. Preheat 13" (33 cm) electric pan or chef pan to 275°F (135°C). Place slices 1" (2.5 cm) apart. Cover with vent open and cook for 20 minutes. Cool on wire racks.

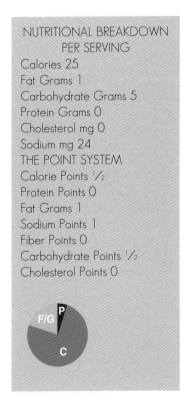

NUTRITIONAL BREAKDOWN
PER SERVING
Calories 25
Fat Grams 1
Carbohydrate Grams 5
Protein Grams 0
Cholesterol mg 0
Sodium mg 24
THE POINT SYSTEM
Calorie Points ½
Protein Points 0
Fat Grams 1
Sodium Points 1
Fiber Points 0
Carbohydrate Points ½
Cholesterol Points 0

CRUST

⅔ cup graham crackers, finely crushed
1 tablespoon sifted powdered sugar
1 tablespoon finely shredded lemon peel
2 tablespoons margarine, melted

FILLING

1 15 ounce (430 g) carton low-fat ricotta cheese
1 8 ounce (230 g) package light cream cheese, softened
1 cup sugar or sugar substitute equivalent
2 tablespoons all-purpose flour
1 tablespoon finely shredded lemon peel
2 tablespoons lemon juice
2 teaspoons vanilla
2 eggs
2 egg whites
1 8 ounce (230 g) carton plain low-fat yogurt

For crust combine crackers, powdered sugar, and lemon peel. Add margarine. Press in bottom of 10" chef pan or large frypan. Cook over low heat for 5 minutes. Cool.

For filling, in a large mixing bowl combine ricotta and cream cheese, sugar, flour, lemon peel, lemon juice and vanilla. Beat with an electric mixer until well blended. Add eggs and egg whites, beating on low speed just until combined. Stir in yogurt. Pour into crust-lined pan. Bake over low heat 1¼ hours or until center appears nearly set when shaken. Chill thoroughly.

Light Cheesecake

Serves: 12 to 14
Preparation Time: 1½ hours

NUTRITIONAL BREAKDOWN
PER SERVING
Calories 176
Fat Grams 3
Carbohydrate Grams 26
Protein Grams 9
Cholesterol mg 39
Sodium mg 344
THE POINT SYSTEM
Calorie Points 2½2
Protein Points 1
Fat Grams 3
Sodium Points 15
Fiber Points
Carbohydrate Points 1½
Cholesterol Points 4

Angel Food Cake

Serves: 10
Preparation Time: 2 hours

1¼   cups (300 ml) eggs whites
      (approximately 7 large eggs)
½   teaspoon salt
1   teaspoon cream of tartar
2   tablespoons water
1½   cups sugar
½   teaspoon vanilla
½   teaspoon almond extract
1   cup cake flour

Beat egg whites and salt in a large bowl at high speed until frothy, about 1 minute. Add cream of tartar. Beat 3 minutes; add water. Continue beating at high speed until whites will stand in peaks, about 3-4 minutes. Turn mixer to low speed; add sugar gradually and flavoring. Beat about ½ minute longer. Sift flour twice and fold in by hand.

Put angel food cake tube in center of 6-quart (6 L) roaster (or make one with slim, tall, heavy glass inverted). Pour batter into dry roaster. Cover with 4-quart (4 L) dome cover. Put on cold, small burner. Turn heat to low. Bake for 50 minutes. DON'T PEEK! LIFTING OF COVER WILL CAUSE CAKE TO FALL. Cake top will cook dry but will not brown.

To cool, place four knife handles evenly under edges of inverted pan. Let cool for 1 hour, then remove cake. Loosen with knife around edge and glass. Lightly brush off loose crumbs.

Serve with Almond Sauce, Chocolate-Marshmallow Sauce or Red Plum Sauce. Recipes on next page.

NUTRITIONAL BREAKDOWN
PER SERVING
Calories 150
Fat Grams 0
Carbohydrate Grams 34
Protein Grams 0
Cholesterol mg 0
Sodium mg 300
THE POINT SYSTEM
Calorie Points 2
Protein Points 0
Fat Grams 0
Sodium Points 13
Fiber Points 0
Carbohydrate Points 2
Cholesterol Points 0

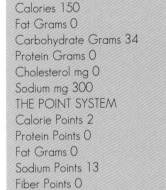

3	tablespoons sugar
2	teaspoons cornstarch
½	cup (120 ml) water
3	tablespoons amaretto
½	teaspoon lemon juice
2	tablespoons sliced almonds
¼	teaspoon almond extract

Combine sugar and cornstarch in a 1-quart saucepan (1.5 L utensil). Stir in water. Place over medium heat and bring to a boil, stirring constantly. Cook 2 minutes or until thickened, stirring constantly.

Stir in amaretto and lemon juice; heat just until mixture comes to a boil. Remove from heat; stir in almonds and extract.

Almond Sauce

Yields: ³/₄ cup
Preparation Time: 15 minutes

Calories 65
Fat Grams 2
Carbohydrate Grams 11
Protein Grams 1
Cholesterol mg 0
Sodium mg 1
Calorie Points 1

⅓	cup miniature marshmallows
2	tablespoons unsweetened cocoa
1	tablespoon cornstarch
1	cup (240 ml) skim milk
1	tablespoon light corn syrup
1	teaspoon vanilla extract
¼	teaspoon ground cinnamon
¼	cup miniature marshmallows
1	tablespoon chopped pecans

Combine ⅓ cup marshmallows, cocoa, and cornstarch in a 1-quart saucepan (1.5 L utensil). Gradually stir in milk and corn syrup. Cook over medium heat, stirring constantly, until thickened, Remove from heat; stir in vanilla and cinnamon. Stir in ¼ cup marshmallows and pecans.

Chocolate-Marshmallow Sauce

Yields: 1 cup
Preparation Time: 15 minutes

Calories 84
Fat Grams 1½
Carbohydrate Grams 17
Protein Grams 3
Cholesterol mg 1
Sodium mg 40
Calorie Points 1

¼	cup sugar
2	teaspoons cornstarch
½	teaspoon ground cinnamon
½	cup (120 ml) peach or apricot nectar
1	cup sliced fresh red plums
½	teaspoon almond extract

Combine sugar, cornstarch and cinnamon in a 2-quart saucepan (2 L utensil); stir well. Add nectar; stir until smooth. Stir in plums. Bring to a boil over medium heat, stirring constantly. Remove from heat and stir in almond extract.

Red Plum Sauce

Yields: 1¹/₃ cups
Preparation Time: 15 minutes

Calories 74
Fat Grams 0
Carbohydrate Grams 19
Protein Grams 0
Cholesterol mg 0
Sodium mg 2
Calorie Points 1

Stovetop Strawberry Shortcake

Serves: 8
Preparation Time: 30 minutes

baking mix
4   cups strawberries
¼   cup sugar
    non-dairy whipped topping

Make shortcake recipe on baking mix box, adding additional sugar. Roll dough out to ½" (1.5 cm) thickness; using 3" (7.5 cm) diameter cookie cutter, cut out shortcakes. Preheat large 13" (33 cm) electric pan or chef pan to 275°F (135°C). Place shortcakes in pan, cover with vent open, bake for 20 minutes. DO NOT PEEK. After cooling, cut shortcakes in half lengthwise.

Meanwhile, halve strawberries after washing and stemming. Place in medium-sized bowl. Sprinkle with sugar to taste. Let sit until shortcakes are cooled. Place bottom half of shortcake on individual serving plate. Spoon 2-3 tablespoons strawberries onto shortcake, place top half of shortcake on top of strawberries, spoon on more strawberries and top with non-dairy whipped cream topping.

NUTRITIONAL BREAKDOWN
PER SERVING
Calories 296
Fat Grams 10
Carbohydrate Grams 50
Protein Grams 3
Cholesterol mg 0
Sodium mg 307
THE POINT SYSTEM
Calorie Points 4
Protein Points 0
Fat Grams 10
Sodium Points 13
Fiber Points 1
Carbohydrate Points 3½
Cholesterol Points 0

2	cups (480 ml) skim milk, divided
1	egg, beaten
3	tablespoons cornstarch
2	tablespoons honey
1	teaspoon vanilla extract
¼	teaspoon orange extract
6	angel food cake slices;
	or ladyfingers, split lengthwise;
	or Twinkies, split lengthwise
1	tablespoon Triple Sec
3	cups fresh strawberries,
	sliced and divided

Combine 1¾ cup (420 ml) milk and egg in a 2-quart saucepan (2 L utensil). Beat with a wire whisk 1 to 2 minutes or until foamy. Combine remaining ¼ cup (60 ml) milk and cornstarch; stir until smooth. Add honey and stir well. Add to milk and egg mixture, and cook over medium heat, stirring constantly, until thickened. Remove from heat and stir in vanilla and orange extracts. Cover and chill.

Arrange half of cake on bottom of trifle dish or clear bowl. Sprinkle cakes with the Triple Sec. Arrange 1 cup sliced strawberries on top of cakes and, cut side out, around lower edge of dish. Top with half of chilled custard and remaining cakes. Repeat with another layer of strawberries. Top with remaining custard and remaining 1 cup strawberries. Cover and chill at least 2 hours. Garnish with whole strawberries, if desired.

Fresh Strawberry Trifle

Serves: 6 or 8
Preparation Time: 2½ hours

NUTRITIONAL BREAKDOWN
PER SERVING
Calories 232
Fat Grams 1
Carbohydrate Grams 48
Protein Grams 7
Cholesterol mg 37
Sodium mg 309
THE POINT SYSTEM
Calorie Points 3
Protein Points 1
Fat Grams 1
Sodium Points 13
Fiber Points 1
Carbohydrate Points 3
Cholesterol Points 4

Raspberry Mash

Serves: 8
Preparation Time: 3 hours

3	tablespoons reduced calorie margarine
2	cups crushed vanilla wafers
1	16 ounce (460 g) bag frozen raspberries, thawed
⅓	cup sugar
⅓	cup (80 ml) skim milk
2	egg yolks
1	envelope unflavored gelatin
½	teaspoon vanilla extract
¼	teaspoon salt
2	egg whites
¼	teaspoon cream of tartar
2	tablespoons sugar
	Fresh raspberries (optional)
	Fresh mint sprigs (optional)

Place margarine in 10" chef pan or large frypan over low heat until melted. Add crushed wafers, stirring well. Press mixture evenly over bottom of pan. Cook over low heat for 10 minutes. Set aside. In 2-quart saucepan (2 L utensil), mash raspberries with masher, add ⅓ cup sugar, skim milk, egg yolks, gelatin, vanilla and salt. Cook over medium heat until boiling; stirring every 2 minutes. Let stand 30-40 minutes or until mixture thickens slightly, or place in refrigerator to cool.

Beat egg whites and cream of tartar at high speed of an electric mixer just until foamy. Gradually add 2 tablespoons sugar, beating until stiff peaks form and sugar dissolves to make a meringue (2-4 minutes). Gently fold raspberry mixture into meringue. Pour mixture into crust. Chill 2 hours or until firm. Garnish with fresh raspberries and mint sprigs.

NUTRITIONAL BREAKDOWN
PER SERVING
Calories 292
Fat Grams 7
Carbohydrate Grams 45
Protein Grams 13
Cholesterol mg 69
Sodium mg 140
THE POINT SYSTEM
Calorie Points 4
Protein Points 2
Fat Grams 7
Sodium Points 6
Fiber Points 1
Carbohydrate Points 3
Cholesterol Points 7

5	whole raw apples
1	tablespoon sugar
¼	teaspoon cinnamon
4	tablespoons butter
1	cup sugar
1	tablespoon water
	sliced almonds for garnish
	raisins for garnish

Baked Apples

Serves: 5
Preparation Time: 50 minutes

Wash apples. Remove cores and blemishes. Pare each apple around the center removing ½" (1.5 cm) of the skin.

Place in 3-quart saucepan (3 L utensil). Mix 1 tablespoon sugar with cinnamon, sprinkle into center of each apple.

Make a syrup with the butter, 1 cup sugar and water. Pour over the apples.

Cover. Place over low heat. Cook 30-40 minutes or until apples are tender. Garnish with sliced almonds and raisins.

NUTRITIONAL BREAKDOWN
PER SERVING
Calories 199
Fat Grams 5
Carbohydrate Grams 41
Protein Grams 0
Cholesterol mg 12
Sodium mg 48
THE POINT SYSTEM
Calorie Points 2½
Protein Points 0
Fat Grams 5
Sodium Points 2
Fiber Points 1½
Carbohydrate Points 3
Cholesterol Points 1

F/G

C

Chocolate Mousse

Serves: 6
Preparation Time: 30 minutes

6	ounces (170 g) semi-sweet chocolate
⅓	cup (80 ml) water
1	tablespoon butter
2	tablespoons rum
3	eggs, separated

Chop the chocolate into small pieces and combine with the water in 2-quart saucepan (2 L utensil). Cook over very low heat so that the chocolate and water form a thick cream. Remove from the heat, allow to cool slightly, and then beat in the butter.

Add the rum and beat in the egg yolks one at a time.

Whip the egg whites until stiff but not dry and fold thoroughly into the chocolate mixture. Pour into small pots or custard cups and chill overnight. Serve topped with whipped cream or fresh raspberries.

NUTRITIONAL BREAKDOWN
PER SERVING
Calories 189
Fat Grams 12
Carbohydrate Grams 19
Protein Grams 3
Cholesterol mg 112
Sodium mg 24
THE POINT SYSTEM
Calorie Points 2½
Protein Points 0
Fat Grams 12
Sodium Points 1
Fiber Points 0
Carbohydrate Points 1
Cholesterol Points 5

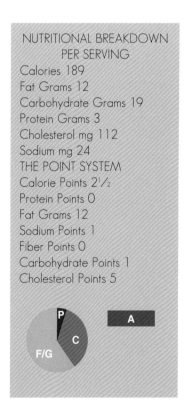

2	cups cake flour
1½	cups sugar
1	tablespoon baking powder
1	teaspoon salt
½	cup (120 ml) canola oil
1½	cups (360 ml) egg substitute (or 1 egg yolk)
¾	cup (180 ml) cold water
1	ripe banana, mashed
1	teaspoon vanilla
6	egg whites
½	teaspoon cream of tarter

GLAZE

powdered sugar
water
bananas, sliced

In large mixing bowl sift together cake flour, sugar, baking powder and salt. Add oil, egg substitute, and water. Mix well using electric mixer. Add banana and vanilla. Beat well.

In separate bowl beat egg whites and cream of tartar to form airy stiff peaks.

Fold banana mixture into egg whites.

Make a tube pan by placing a tall glass inverted into center of 6-quart (6 L) roaster. Pour mixture around glass. Cover with 4-quart (4 L) dome cover. Place on cold burner, turn to medium heat for 5 minutes; reduce to low for 55 minutes. Cake is dove when a toothpick is inserted and removed cleanly. Remove from heat, invert pan to cool using center glass as a stand. Cool 30 minutes. Run knife around edges and center glass, invert cake onto plate to serve and remove glass.

Or pour mixture into ungreased tube or bundt pan and bake at 350°F (180°C) for 45-55 minutes. Invert to cool.

Glaze with thin icing of powdered sugar and water. Add sliced bananas to top if desired.

Banana Chiffon Cake

Serves: 12
Preparation Time: 1 hour, 15 minutes

NUTRITIONAL BREAKDOWN
PER SERVING
Calories 267
Fat Grams 10
Carbohydrate Grams 42
Protein Grams 4
Cholesterol mg 18
Sodium mg 279
THE POINT SYSTEM
Calorie Points 3½
Protein Points 0
Fat Grams 10
Sodium Points 12
Fiber Points 0
Carbohydrate Points 2½
Cholesterol Points 2

Serves: 12
Preparation Time: 35 minutes

Pineapple Upside-Down Cake

1	20 ounce (570 g) can sliced pineapple (reserve liquid)
1	package yellow cake mix
⅓	cup butter
¾	cup brown sugar
	maraschino cherries
	heavy cream, whipped (optional)

Drain pineapple juice into measuring cup. Mix cake according to package directions, using reserved pineapple juice for the liquid. In large frypan, melt butter over medium low heat, add brown sugar spread evenly over bottom of pan. Arrange pineapple, place cherry in center of each slice, add beaten cake mixture so pan is two-thirds full. Cover with 4-quart (4 L) dome cover, form a water seal over medium heat, (approximately 7 minutes). Reduce to low, bake 25 minutes. Remove cover quickly so condensed moisture does not drip back on cake.

Invert large platter over pan and turn quickly. Lift pan gently from cake. Serve warm or cold with or without whipped cream topping.

Variation
Apricot Upside-Down Cake

See Pineapple Upside-Down Cake
on page 192.

Serves: 12
Preparation Time: 1 hour

1	stick (115 g) butter or margarine
1	cup light brown sugar
2	14.5 ounce (410 g) cans apricot halves, drained and juice reserved
1	8 ounce (230 g) can crushed pineapple, drained and juice reserved
1	teaspoon cinnamon
½	teaspoon nutmeg
1	stick (115 g) butter or margarine
1	cup sugar
2	eggs
1	cup flour, sifted
1½	teaspoons baking powder
½	teaspoon baking soda
½	teaspoon salt
½	cup (120 ml) buttermilk
1	teaspoon vanilla

In 13" (33 cm) electric pan or chef pan, melt butter covering sides of pan. Add brown sugar and ½ cup (120 ml) apricot juice to butter, simmer about 5 minutes or until slightly thickened. Arrange apricot halves in pan, sprinkle crushed pineapple over apricots, sprinkle with cinnamon and nutmeg.

In a bowl, cream butter and sugar, add eggs one at a time, mixing well. Mix dry ingredients together. Alternately add dry ingredients and buttermilk, mix well. Add vanilla last. Drop mixture by spoonfuls over fruit and smooth over the top. Cover and cook over low heat 45 minutes. Cool slightly, invert onto platter and serve warm with ice cream.

Carrot Cake with Cream Cheese Frosting

Serves: 16
Preparation Time: 1 hour

  ❖

NUTRITIONAL BREAKDOWN
PER SERVING
Calories 338
Fat Grams 9
Carbohydrate Grams 63
Protein Grams 3
Cholesterol mg 1
Sodium mg 158
THE POINT SYSTEM
Calorie Points 5
Protein Points 0
Fat Grams 9
Sodium Points 7
Fiber Points 0
Carbohydrate Points 4
Cholesterol Points 0

CARROT CAKE

1¾ cups all-purpose flour
1¼ cups sugar
½ cup oat or wheat bran
1 teaspoon baking powder
1 teaspoon baking soda
1 teaspoon cinnamon
3 cups carrots, finely shredded
⅔ cup (160 ml) oil or applesauce
3 egg whites
¼ cup (60 ml) corn syrup

Coat a 10" chef pan or large frypan with non-stick spray. Combine flour, sugar, oat or wheat bran, baking powder, baking soda, and cinnamon. Add carrots, cooking oil (or applesauce), egg whites, and corn syrup. Beat with an electric mixer till thoroughly combined. Pour batter into the prepared pan. Cover and bake on top of stove on low heat for 45 minutes-1 hour or until a wooden toothpick inserted near the center comes out clean. Invert cake pan on plate. While cooling mix cream cheese frosting. Allow cake to cool then frost or frost while still warm to glaze. Cover cake and store in refrigerator.

CREAM CHEESE FROSTING

½ cup fat-free cream cheese
3¼ cups powdered sugar, separated
2 teaspoons vanilla
½ teaspoon grated lemon
  or orange peel

In a medium bowl beat together cream cheese, 2 cups powdered sugar, vanilla, and grated lemon or orange peel until light and fluffy. Gradually beat in about 1¼ cups powdered sugar until consistency to spread.

1	cup low fat margarine or butter
1¼	cups brown sugar, packed
2	eggs
1	teaspoon vanilla
1	teaspoon baking soda
½	teaspoon salt
2	cups rolled oats
2¼	cups flour, unbleached
1	12 ounce (345 g) bag chocolate chips

Chocolate Chip Cookie Bars

Yields: 24
Preparation Time: 40 minutes

Cream margarine or butter with the brown sugar. Add the eggs and vanilla and blend. Add the baking soda, salt, rolled oats and flour together. Add the flour mixture into the creamed mixture and blend. Add the chocolate chips and blend gently.

Using the 13" (33 cm) electric pan or chef pan, press the mixture into the bottom of the utensil. Turn the thermostat to 200°F (90°C) and cook for 25 minutes, covered with vent open. Let rest in utensil for 5 minutes before carefully cutting and serving. In chef pan, cover, place over medium heat 5 minutes, reduce to low for 25 minutes. (Or place mixture onto a cookie sheet and bake in 350°F (180°C) oven for 12 minutes.)

NUTRITIONAL BREAKDOWN
PER SERVING
Calories 217
Fat Grams 8
Carbohydrate Grams 36
Protein Grams 3
Cholesterol mg 0
Sodium mg 195
THE POINT SYSTEM
Calorie Points 3
Protein Points 0
Fat Grams 8
Sodium Points 8
Fiber Points 0
Carbohydrate Points 2½
Cholesterol Points 0

Rice Pudding

Serves: 4
Preparation Time: 30 minutes

1	cup rice
1½	cups (360 ml) milk
1	vanilla bean
	pinch of salt
	raisins (optional)
½	cup granulated sugar
1	egg

Wash and drain the rice. Pour into a 3-quart saucepan (3 L utensil); add enough water to cover rice; cover pan. Bring to a boil over medium-high heat. As soon as the water has been absorbed (about 10 minutes), add milk, vanilla bean, and salt. Raisins can be added if desired.

Cover, reduce to medium-low heat and cook for 10 minutes.

Remove from heat, add the sugar and egg. Cover, and let stand to finish cooking completely (approximately 5 minutes) before serving.

NUTRITIONAL BREAKDOWN
PER SERVING
Calories 187
Fat Grams 0
Carbohydrate Grams 41
Protein Grams 5
Cholesterol mg 2
Sodium mg 62
THE POINT SYSTEM
Calorie Points 2¹/₂
Protein Points 1
Fat Grams 0
Sodium Points 3
Fiber Points 0
Carbohydrate Points 2¹/₂
Cholesterol Points 0

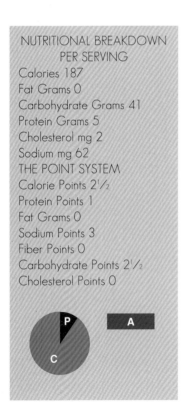

Caramel Flan

CARAMEL
½   cup sugar
¼   cup (60 ml) water

CUSTARD
4   eggs, slightly beaten
6   tablespoons sugar
2   cups (480 ml) half-n-half (half milk, half cream)
1   teaspoon vanilla
1   cup (240 ml) water

Combine the sugar and water for caramel in a 1-quart saucepan (1.5 L utensil). Place on low heat and stir until sugar is completely dissolved. After all sugar is dissolved, increase to high heat, continue to stir until syrup turns a deep golden color. Remove from heat and pour into inset pan. Tip and turn inset pan to coat evenly the bottom and sides.

Beat all of the other ingredients together for the custard. Pour into caramelized inset pan. Cover inset pan tightly with aluminum foil. Add 2 cups (480 ml) water to 6-quart (6 L) roaster with steamer rack. Set inset pan on top of rack, cover with 4-quart (4 L) dome cover. Turn to medium high heat. Form a water seal, then reduce to medium heat. Continue to cook for 45 minutes. Remove from heat. Remove foil, allow to cool, then refrigerate. Place a serving dish (large enough to accommodate the caramel sauce) over the mold and invert. Serve completely chilled. Can be garnished with orange or lemon zest or fresh fruit.

Cooks tip: To make the caramel, once the sugar has dissolved, turn to high heat to caramelize and watch closely. Medium heat allows too much moisture to escape, causing syrup to become granular again.

Serves: 8
Preparation Time: 3 hours

NUTRITIONAL BREAKDOWN
PER SERVING
Calories 174
Fat Grams 7
Carbohydrate Grams 25
Protein Grams 4
Cholesterol mg 22
Sodium mg 52
THE POINT SYSTEM
Calorie Points 2½
Protein Points 0
Fat Grams 7
Sodium Points 2
Fiber Points 0
Carbohydrate Points 1½
Cholesterol Points 2

Bread Pudding

Serves: 8
Preparation Time: 30 minutes

4	1" (2.5 cm) slices French bread, cubed
2	cups (480 ml) skim milk
⅓	cup brown sugar, packed
1	tablespoon butter
½	cup raisins
3	eggs, lightly beaten
1	teaspoon cinnamon
½	teaspoon salt
½	teaspoon vanilla
2	teaspoons orange zest, chopped
2	cups (480 ml) water

Dry bread cubes in low temperature oven 200°F (90°C) for 20 minutes, or dry overnight at room temperature. Heat milk, sugar, butter, and raisins in saucepan. Put eggs, cinnamon, salt, vanilla and zest in bowl and whisk to combine. Whisk in hot milk mixture and add bread cubes. Stir for about 20 seconds, pushing bread cubes into hot liquid. Do not stir longer or bread will become too soft.

Pour mixture into inset pan. Pour 2 cups (480 ml) water into 3-quart saucepan (3 L utensil), place inset pan in pan with water, cover, place over medium heat for 30 minutes.

Serve with Rum or Piña Colada Sauce.

Rum Sauce

1	stick (115 g) butter
½	cup sugar
¼	cup (60 ml) dark rum

Melt butter in 1-quart saucepan (1.5 L utensil), add sugar and cook for 5 minutes over medium heat, stirring constantly. Remove from heat and add remaining ingredients. Return to medium heat and cook for 1 minute.

Piña Colada Sauce

1	stick (115 g) butter
½	cup sugar
1	teaspoon pineapple extract
1	teaspoon coconut extract
¼	cup coconut flakes
¼	cup pineapple chunks

Follow directions above.

NUTRITIONAL BREAKDOWN
PER SERVING
(not including sauce)
Calories 137
Fat Grams 2
Carbohydrate Grams 26
Protein Grams 5
Cholesterol mg 5
Sodium mg 147
THE POINT SYSTEM
Calorie Points 2
Protein Points ½
Fat Grams 2
Sodium Points 6
Fiber Points 0
Carbohydrate Points 1½
Cholesterol Points 0

butter or non-stick cooking spray
1¼   cups unsifted all purpose flour
¾   cup sugar
2   teaspoons baking powder
½   teaspoon salt
¼   cup shortening
⅔   cup (160 ml) skim milk
1   egg
1   teaspoon vanilla

Easy One-Egg Cake

Serves: 12
Preparation Time: 30 minutes

Generously butter 8" chef pan or small frypan. In large mixing bowl, combine flour, sugar, baking powder, salt, shortening, and milk. Blend well at low speed. Beat 1½ minutes at medium speed. Add egg and vanilla; continue beating 1½ minutes at medium speed. Pour batter into pan. Cook on low heat for 18 minutes with the cover on. Cake will be golden brown, and the top springs back when lightly touched. Invert onto plate.

After cake has been inverted, frost by placing a chocolate candy bar* on top to melt, spreading with knife.

* For chocolate candy nutrition refer to wrapper.

NUTRITIONAL BREAKDOWN
PER SERVING
Calories 142
Fat Grams 4
Carbohydrate Grams 23
Protein Grams 2
Cholesterol mg 0
Sodium mg 149
THE POINT SYSTEM
Calorie Points 2
Protein Points 0
Fat Grams 4
Sodium Points 7
Fiber Points 0
Carbohydrate Points 1½
Cholesterol Points 0

Garam Masala

1   bay leaf
1/2   teaspoon whole black pepper
1/2   teaspoon whole cloves
1/2   teaspoon cinnamon stick
1/2   teaspoon cardamom

Garam Masala is simply a blend of fresh roasted spices. Individually dry roast each spice over medium heat until fragrant. Then using a coffee grinder (used for spices only) or a mortar and pestle, grind the spices together.

Indian Curry Spice Mix

1/2   cup coriander seeds
1/4   cup cumin seeds
8   dried red chilies, seeded
1   tablespoon peppercorns
1   tablespoon black mustard seeds
2   tablespoons turmeric
2   tablespoons fenugreek

Individually dry roast first five spices. Grind to fine. Mix all ingredients together. Store spice mixture in a jar in a dark place, not the refrigerator. Keeps approximately 3 months.

5-Spice Mix

1   tablespoon whole fennel seeds
1   tablespoon star anise
1   cinnamon stick
1   tablespoon whole cloves
1   tablespoon Szechhuan
      pepper corns

Dry roast in 8" chef pan or small frypan, one spice at a time. Grind in spice grinder or use a mortar and pestle.

Roasted Rice Powder

Heat a 8" chef pan or small frypan over medium-high heat. Add 1/4 cup raw rice, preferably glutinous rice, and stir constantly as rice heats. After several minutes it will have a lightly toasted aroma and will begin to turn pale brown. Keep stirring until all the rice has changed to a light tan color, then transfer to a spice grinder or a large mortar and pestle and grind to a fine powder. Roasted rice powder keeps well in a sealed glass jar for several months. Use as needed in Thai and Vietnamese dishes.

Bouquet Garni

Equal portions of:
     dried dill weed
     thyme
     basil
     parsley
     marjoram
     tarragon.

A mixture of herbs (tied by the stems or placed in a cloth bag,) to flavor a broth or stew and then removed before serving.

Tahini

Tahini is available in Middle Eastern and some health food stores. You can make your own by grinding sesame seeds and adding enough sesame oil to give the mixture the consistency of peanut butter.

Blanched Almonds

Cover almonds with 1 cup water, bring to boil, turn off heat, and soak overnight (at least 4-5 hours.) Drain, peel outer skin, and slice lengthwise.

The Surgeons General Report on Nutrition and Health, 1988, U.S. Department of Health and Human Services, Washington D.C. 20402.

Calorie Point Diet – a "point" in the right direction toward weight management, Still Regional Medical Center, Jefferson City, Missouri.

Fit or Fat, Baily, Covert; Houton Mifflin Co., Boston, 1977.

The Dieter's Dilemma, Bennet, William, M.D.; Gwin, Joel; Basic Books, Inc., New York, 1982.

Eating is OK, Jordon, Henry A., M.D.; Levitz, Leonard, Ph.D.; Kimbrell, Gordon, M., Ph.D.; Signet 1978.

Exercise Physiology, McArdle, William D.; Katch, Frank I.; Victor L.; Lea and Febiger, Philadelphia, 1981.

Fiber, Swartz, Roni, R.D.; Nutrition Information Center of Osteopathic Hospital, 2622 W. Central, Wichita, KS, 1983.

Professional Guide to HCF Diets, James W. Anderson, M.D.; F.A.C.P. Beverling Sieling, R.D.; Wen-Ju Leu Chen, Ph.D.; Lexington, Kentucky, 1981. (Published by HCF Diabetes Research Foundation, Inc., 1872 Blaermore Rd., Lexington, Kentucky.)

Food Values of Portions Commonly Used, Jean A.T. Pennington and Helen Nichols Church, Harper & Row Publishers, New York, 13th Edition.

Wesley Calorie Point Book, Nutrition Department, HCS Wesley Medical Center, 550 N. Hillside, Wichita, Kansas.